DATE DUE

D1367107

Careers
in Focus

Social Work

Ferguson Publishing Company
Chicago, Illinois

Andrew Morkes, *Managing Editor-Career Publications*
Carol Yehling, *Senior Editor*
Anne Paterson, *Editor*
Nora Walsh, *Assistant Editor*
Paula Garner, *Additional Editorial Assistance*

Library of Congress Cataloging-in-Publication Data

Careers in focus. Social work.
    p. cm. -- (Careers in focus)
Includes index.
  ISBN 0-89434-405-6
  1. Social service--Vocational guidance--Juvenile literature. [1.
Social service--Vocational guidance. 2. Vocational guidance.] I. Title:
Social work. II. Series.
  HV10.5 .C38 2001
  361.3'2'02373--dc21

                                    2001004149

Printed in the United States of America

Cover photo courtesy Ronnie Kaufman/The Stock Market

Published and distributed by
Ferguson Publishing Company
200 West Jackson Boulevard, 7th Floor
Chicago, Illinois 60606
800-306-9941
www.fergpubco.com

Table of Contents

Introduction

There are four categories of social services: individual and family services, residential care, job training and vocational rehabilitation services, and miscellaneous social services.

Individual and family services provide counseling and welfare services, including refugee, disaster, and temporary relief aid. This category includes the government offices that supply welfare assistance, rent supplements, and food stamps. It also includes agencies that provide adult day care, and in-home services such as delivered meals, home health care, and chore services. Other services are child-oriented, such as big brother/big sister programs, child protective services, and adoption services. Counseling offered by crisis centers is also a part of this area of social work.

Residential care is round-the-clock personal and social care (excluding medical care) provided for the homeless, runaways, children, the elderly, alcohol and drug abusers, the mentally ill, the developmentally disabled, and others who are unable to care for themselves.

Job training and vocational rehabilitation services help the unemployed, disabled, and poorly educated learn new job skills or find jobs that fit their current skills.

Miscellaneous social services include groups that focus on social change and community improvement, such as advocacy groups, health and welfare councils, and antipoverty boards. They work at the administrative level to change social policy and raise and distribute funds to appropriate agencies.

Shelters demonstrate the variety of jobs available in social services, from helping someone budget for rent and groceries, to building a house for a homeless family, to campaigning for funds and writing grant proposals.

Before a shelter can open, policymakers conduct research through surveys, interviews, and evaluations. They decide how to operate and finance the program. They answer questions such as: Is there a need for the shelter? Where is the best location? How many people will be served? How many people will be employed? Where can the money come from? What services will be available? and What impact will the shelter have on the neighborhood? Fund-raisers and grant writers investigate the financial resources available for the project. Once funding is awarded and operating expenses can be met, the fund-monitoring staff keeps track of the money, a key aspect to the continuing survival of an organization.

Publicity is necessary for a shelter to inform the community of the services available and to convey the quality and success of the program. A community outreach director will work to educate the community about the problem of teen runaways. A public relations specialist may post notices about the shelter in areas frequented by runaways.

A shelter needs people to work directly with clients. Counselors and therapists conduct individual and group sessions. They also manage hotlines, providing counseling in crisis situations. Social workers or psychologists will work with individuals to help them return to school or their homes, or to help prepare them for a foster home. These professionals also will evaluate client needs, and possibly recommend an extended program of service.

A staff at a shelter might include tutors to conduct individual lessons and study groups or trainers to help runaways get involved in school or community sports teams. Employee assistance personnel might provide job counseling, interview skills, and special training.

Shelters also require security guards, live-in residential assistants, a custodial crew, cooks, and other positions.

According to the U.S. Department of Labor, opportunities in social services should be numerous through 2008. Predicted growth rates for the various segments of the industry range from 31 percent in job training and vocational rehabilitation services to 57 percent in residential care. Many job openings should arise in large occupations with easier entry, relatively low pay, and high turnover, such as home health and personal care aides.

Every community recognizes the importance of social services. New social problems develop every day that demand attention. Government funding, however, is necessary for most social programs to survive, and bureaucracy and budget cuts often make it difficult to keep a social service in operation. New initiatives in job retraining and welfare reform could brighten prospects for social services workers, but much depends on government policies.

There are increasing opportunities in the private sector, such as in drug rehabilitation, marriage counseling, and career counseling. Public sector jobs will continue to have a high demand for social services workers, particularly in large metropolitan areas.

As client groups change, so will social services. For example, as gays and lesbians continue to assert their civil rights and to seek legislation protecting them from discrimination, the social services worker will become more involved in providing them advocacy and legal aid. Changes in immigration policies also will change the kinds of social services available to legal and illegal immigrants.

More social services will be made available to the elderly as our population grows older. More people will be in need of these services as they live longer and as the baby boom generation reaches retirement age. The type of services provided to the elderly is also changing. Home care will be in higher demand, as the next generation of elderly will most likely prefer care in their own homes over care in retirement communities.

Each article in this book discusses a particular social work occupation in detail. The articles in *Careers in Focus: Social Work* appear in Ferguson's *Encyclopedia of Careers and Vocational Guidance,* but have been updated and revised with the latest information from the U.S. Department of Labor and other sources. Additionally, a new article (Nonprofit Social Service Directors) has been specifically written for this book. The **Overview** section is a brief introductory description of the duties and responsibilities of someone in the career. Oftentimes, a career may have a variety of job titles. When this is the case, alternative career titles are presented in this section. The **History** section describes the history of the particular job as it relates to the overall development of its industry or field. **The Job** describes the primary and secondary duties of the job. **Requirements** discusses high school and postsecondary education and training requirements, any certification or licensing necessary, and any other personal requirements for success in the job. **Exploring** offers suggestions on how to gain some experience in or knowledge of the particular job before making a firm educational and financial commitment. The focus is on what can be done while still in high school (or in the early years of college) to gain a better understanding of the job. The **Employers** section gives an overview of typical places of employment for the job. **Starting Out** discusses the best ways to land that first job, be it through the college placement office, newspaper ads, or personal contact. The **Advancement** section describes what kind of career path to expect from the job and how to get on it. **Earnings** lists salary ranges and describes the typical fringe benefits. The **Work Environment** section describes the typical surroundings and conditions of employment, whether indoors or outdoors, noisy or quiet, social or independent, and so on. Also discussed are typical hours worked, any seasonal fluctuations, and the stresses and strains of the job. The **Outlook** section summarizes the job in terms of the general economy and industry projections. For the most part, Outlook information is obtained from the Bureau of Labor Statistics and is supplemented by information taken from professional associations. Job growth terms follow those used in the *Occupational Outlook Handbook.* Growth described as "much faster than the average" means an increase of 36 percent or more. Growth described as "faster than the average" means an increase of 21 to 35 percent. Growth described as "about as fast as the average" means an increase of 10 to 20 percent. Growth described as "little change or more slowly than the average" means an increase of 0 to 9 percent. "Decline" means a decrease of 1 percent or more. Each article ends with **For More Information,** which lists organizations that can provide career information on training, education, internships, scholarships, and job placement.

Adult Day Care Coordinators

	School Subjects
Family and consumer science Psychology Sociology	
	Personal Skills
Helping/teaching Leadership/management	
	Work Environment
Primarily indoors Primarily one location	
	Minimum Education Level
Associate's degree	
	Salary Range
$18,000 to $31,000 to $45,000	
	Certification or Licensing
Required for certain positions	
	Outlook
Much faster than the average	

Overview

Adult day care coordinators direct day care programs for adults—usually elderly or disabled—who cannot be left alone all day. They oversee staff members who provide care, meals, and social activities to day care clients and serve as a liaison between the day care center and its clients' families.

History

Adult day care had its beginnings in the 1940s in psychiatric hospitals. It started as an effort to help patients who had been released from mental institutions. Over the next 20 years the focus gradually shifted from psychiatric care to other kinds of health maintenance. The landmark publication, *Developing Day Care for Older People,* published by the National Council on

Aging (NCOA) in 1972, provided technical assistance for establishing adult day care, and by 1978 there were nearly 300 adult day care centers throughout the United States.

In the 1980s the first Congressional hearing was held on adult day care programs and the Economic Recovery Act was passed, allowing a tax credit to families with elderly members in day care. NCOA established voluntary standards.

There are now more than 4,000 adult day centers currently operating in the United States. Approximately 90 percent operate on a nonprofit or public basis and many are affiliated with larger organizations such as home care, skilled nursing facilities, medical centers, or multipurpose senior organizations.

The Job

Adult day care coordinators direct adult day care centers. Although specific duties vary depending upon the size of the center and the services it offers, the general responsibility of coordinators is to ensure that their centers provide the necessary care for clients. Such care may include attention to personal hygiene and providing meals, medications and therapies, and social activities.

Although coordinators working in small day care centers may actually perform some services for clients, this is not the norm. Instead, coordinators usually oversee various staff members who provide the caregiving. A large center, for example, might have a nurse, physical therapist, social worker, cook, and several aides. Coordinators are responsible for staff hiring, training, and scheduling. They may meet with staff members either one-on-one or in group sessions to review and discuss plans for the clients.

Overseeing meal planning and preparation is also the responsibility of the adult day care coordinator. In most centers, clients are given a midday meal and usually juices and snacks in the mornings and afternoons. Coordinators work with a cook or dietitian to develop well-rounded menus that take into account the nutritional needs of the clients, including any particular restrictions such as diabetic or low-sodium diets. The coordinator may also oversee purchasing and taking inventory of the center's food supply.

The coordinator schedules daily and weekly activities for the day care clients. Depending upon the particular needs and abilities of the clients, a recreational schedule might include crafts, games, exercises, reading time, or movies. In some centers, clients are taken on outings to shopping centers, parks, or restaurants. The coordinator plans such outings, arranging for transportation and any reservations or special accommodations that may be necessary. Finally, the coordinator also organizes parties for special events, such as holidays or birthdays.

Finding new activities and visitors for the center is also part of the job. Coordinators might recruit volunteers to teach crafts or music to the clients. Often, church or civic groups also visit such facilities to visit with clients. Some such groups institute "buddy" programs, in which each group member pairs with a day care client to develop an ongoing relationship. The day care coordinator must authorize and monitor any group visits, activities, or programs.

In addition to planning and overseeing the activities of the center and its clients, the adult day care coordinator also works closely with client family members to make sure that each individual is receiving care that best fits his or her needs. This relationship with the clients' families usually begins before the client is placed in the day care center.

When a family is considering placing an elderly relative in day care, they often have many questions about the center and its activities. The coordinator meets with family members to show them the center and explain to them how it is run. The coordinator also gathers information about the potential client, including names and phone numbers of doctors and people to contact in case of emergency; lists of medications taken with instructions on when and how they should be administered; and information on allergies, food choices, and daily habits and routines.

After the client is placed in the center, the coordinator may meet periodically with the client's family to update them on how the client is responding to the day care setting. If necessary, the coordinator may advise the family about social services, such as home health care, and refer them to other providers.

Adult day care coordinators may have other duties, depending upon the center and how it is owned and operated. For example, they may be responsible for developing and adhering to a budget for the center. In centers licensed or certified by the state, coordinators may ensure that their centers remain in compliance with the regulations and necessary documentation. They may also be responsible for general bookkeeping, bill payment, and office management.

In addition to supervising centers, coordinators may also promote and advertise to the community. They may help with fund-raising, prepare press releases, and speak to various service clubs.

Requirements

High School

Although the vast majority of employers require at least a high school diploma, there are no definite educational requirements for becoming an adult day care coordinator. Some people learn their skills on the job; others have taken courses in home nursing or health care. High school students who are considering a career as an adult day care coordinator should take classes in psychology, sociology, and home economics. Because communication is an important skill, English and speech classes are also good choices.

Postsecondary Training

Many employers prefer to hire candidates who meet the standards set by the National Adult Day Services Association. In order to meet these standards, a coordinator must have a bachelor's degree in health or social services or a related field, with one year's supervisory experience in a social or health services setting. In preparation for such a career, a college student might choose occupational, recreational, or rehabilitation therapy or social work. An increasingly popular major for potential adult day care coordinators is gerontology, or geriatrics.

More than 600 colleges and universities in the United States offer a formal program of instruction in gerontology. Although specific courses vary from school to school, most programs consist of classes in social gerontology, biology and physiology of aging, psychology of aging, and sociology of aging. In addition to these four core classes, most programs offer elective courses in such areas as social policy, community services, nutrition and exercise, diversity in aging, health issues, death and dying, and ethics and life extension.

A practicum or field placement is also a part of most gerontology programs. This allows students to obtain experience working with both well-functioning elderly people and those with age-related disabilities.

Certification or Licensing

No certification or licensing is required to become an adult day care coordinator. In some cases, however, the agency that a coordinator works for may be licensed or certified by the state health department. Any adult day care center that receives payment from Medicare or from other government agencies must be certified by the state department of health. In these cases, licensing requirements may include requirements for coordinators and other staff members. The trend is toward stricter standards.

Other Requirements

Regardless of what level of education a prospective coordinator has, there are certain personal characteristics that are necessary for success in this field. Compassion and an affinity for the elderly and disabled are vital, as are patience and the desire to help others.

Exploring

There are several ways for high school students to learn more about the career of adult day care coordinator. The first and easiest way is to visit a nursing home or adult day care center in order to experience firsthand what it is like to spend time with and interact with elderly people. It might even be wise to take a volunteer position or part-time job in such a facility. This would allow you to gauge your aptitude for a career in aging.

You might also check your local library for books or articles on aging in order to learn more about this career.

Employers

Adult day care coordinators work at adult day care centers. These may be small or large. It is estimated that there are more than 4,000 adult day care centers currently operating in the United States. Most of them are operated on a nonprofit or public basis, and many are affiliated with large organizations such as nursing homes, hospitals, or multipurpose senior organizations. Standards and work environments will vary.

Starting Out

In looking for a position as an adult day care coordinator, candidates should first locate and contact all such programs in the area. Checking the local yellow pages under "Nursing Homes," "Residential Care Facilities," "Aging Services," or "Senior Citizens Services" should provide a list of leads. The job seeker might either send a resume and cover letter or call these potential employers directly. Prospective coordinators should also watch for job openings listed in area newspapers.

Another means of finding job leads is to become affiliated with a professional association, such as the American Geriatrics Society, the American Association of Homes and Services for the Aging, the Gerontological Society of America, or the National Council on Aging. Many such organizations have monthly or quarterly newsletters that list job opportunities. Some may even have job banks or referral services.

Job seekers who have received associate's or bachelor's degrees should also check with the career placement offices at their colleges or universities.

Advancement

Because the field of aging-related services continues to grow, the potential for advancement for adult day care coordinators is good. Some coordinators advance by transferring to a larger center that pays better wages. Others may eventually start their own centers. Still others advance by moving into management positions in other, similar social service organizations, such as nursing homes, hospices, or government agencies on aging.

Finally, an adult day care coordinator might choose to return to school and complete a higher degree—often a master's degree in social work. For those who choose this option, there are many career opportunities in the field of social services. Social workers might, for example, work with individuals and families dealing with AIDS, cancer, or other debilitating illnesses. They might also work for agencies offering various types of counseling, rehabilitation, or crisis intervention.

Earnings

Starting salaries for this position depend partly upon the experience and education of the coordinator and partly upon the size and location of the day care center. Larger centers located in metropolitan areas tend to offer the highest wages.

According to the Association for Gerontology in Higher Education, beginning annual salaries range from $18,000 to $31,000 for persons with a bachelor's degree and little experience. Generally, coordinators who do not have a bachelor's degree can expect to earn somewhat less than this. Experienced coordinators with a bachelor's degree employed in large, well-funded centers may earn from $20,000 to $45,000 annually.

In addition to salary, some coordinators are also offered a benefits package, which typically includes health insurance, paid vacation and sick days, and a retirement plan.

Work Environment

Most adult day care centers have a schedule that corresponds to standard business hours. Most coordinators work a 40-hour week, Monday through Friday, with weekends off.

The coordinator's work environment will vary depending upon the size and type of center he or she supervises. Some centers are fairly institutional, resembling children's day care centers or nursing homes. Others have a more residential feel, being carpeted and furnished like a private home. Regardless of the furnishings, the center is typically clean, well lit, and equipped with ramps, rails, and other devices that ensure the safety of clients.

Part of the coordinator's day may be spent in the center's common areas with clients and staff. He or she may also spend time working in an on-site office. If the staff members take clients on outings, the coordinator may accompany them.

Coordinators are on their feet much of the time, ensuring that meals and activities run smoothly and helping staff members when necessary. Attire for the job varies from center to center, ranging from very casual to standard office wear. Most coordinators, however, wear clothing that is comfortable and allows them freedom of movement.

Regardless of the size of the center, coordinators spend the majority of their time working with people—both staff members and day care clients. Working with clients is often very trying. Many of them may have had a stroke or have Alzheimer's disease, and they may be confused, uncooperative, and even hostile. The job may also be emotionally taxing for the coordinator who becomes attached to his or her clients. Most adults who use a day care center are elderly or permanently disabled; for this reason, day care staff must frequently deal with the decline and eventual death of their clients.

Outlook

The career outlook for adult day care coordinators, as for all human services workers, is expected to be excellent through 2008. According to the U.S. Department of Labor, the number of human services workers is projected to grow by 53 percent between the years 1998 and 2008, with adult day care, specifically, being one of the fastest-growing human services areas.

The main reason for this is that the senior citizen population is growing rapidly. Currently, there are 34 million Americans over the age of 65; by 2030, there will be more than 69 million. This rapid growth has led to the development and increased popularity of aging-related services over the last several years. The increase in adult day care centers is one example of this trend. According to the National Adult Day Services Association, there were as few as 15 adult day care centers in existence in the 1970s; today, there are more than 4,000. This growth should continue as Americans become increasingly aware of the diverse needs of the elderly and the various service options available to them. Adult day care is expected to be used more frequently as a cost-efficient and preferable alternative to nursing homes.

For More Information

For information on aging, services for the elderly, and careers in gerontology, contact the following organizations:

American Association of Homes and Services for the Aging
901 E Street, NW, Suite 500
Washington, DC 20004-2011
Tel: 202-783-2242
Web: http://www.aahsa.org

American Geriatrics Society
350 Fifth Avenue, Suite 801
New York, NY 10118
Tel: 212-308-1414
Email: info@americangeriatrics.org
Web: http://www.americangeriatrics.org

Association for Gerontology in Higher Education
1030 15th Street, NW, Suite 240
Washington, DC 20005-1503
Tel: 202-289-9806
Email: aghetemp@aghe.org
Web: http://www.aghe.org

Gerontological Society of America
1030 15th Street, NW, Suite 250
Washington, DC 20005
Tel: 202-842-1275
Web: http://www.geron.org

National Association of Area Agencies on Aging
927 15th Street, NW, Sixth Floor
Washington, DC 20005
Tel: 202-296-8130
Web: http://www.n4a.org

National Council on the Aging
409 Third Street, SW
Washington, DC 20024
Tel: 202-479-1200
Email: info@ncoa.org
Web: http://www.ncoa.org

Alcohol and Drug Abuse Counselors

School Subjects
Health
Psychology
Sociology

Personal Skills
Communication/ideas
Helping/teaching

Work Environment
Primarily indoors
Primarily one location

Minimum Education Level
Associate's degree

Salary Range
$27,336 to $33,740 to $48,742+

Certification or Licensing
Required by certain states

Outlook
Much faster than the average

Overview

Alcohol and drug abuse counselors work with people who abuse or are addicted to drugs or alcohol. Through individual and group counseling sessions, they help their clients understand and change their destructive substance abuse behaviors.

History

Throughout history people have used drugs for a variety of purposes—for healing, for religious ceremonies, to alter consciousness for self-understanding, to loosen inhibitions and have fun, or to dull the senses against emotional or physical pain. Alcohol and other substances were used in ancient Egypt, Greece, and India as offerings to spiritual beings, as well as to reach a higher consciousness. Many religions today, from Tibetan Buddhism to Roman Catholicism, use alcohol in traditional ceremonies.

Throughout the ages people have abused drugs and alcohol, too. No matter what the purpose for the initial drug use, it becomes for some people an obsession, and then an addiction. The history of treatment for substance abuse is much shorter. In the 1800s, alcoholics and morphine addicts were placed in asylums. Treatments sometimes included miracle medicines that were supposed to be quick "cures" for addicts. In the early 1900s doctors used electroshock therapies and psychosurgery to treat alcoholics.

In 1935, the Alcoholics Anonymous (AA) program was started by two men known as Bill and Dr. Bob. They helped each other achieve sobriety and continued to help others. This system of alcoholics helping other alcoholics grew into the AA movement, which is still strong today. The 12-step program has been adapted and used effectively to treat addictions of all kinds.

Today alcohol and a huge variety of dangerous drugs are readily available—marijuana, cocaine, LSD, heroin, inhalants, amphetamines, barbiturates, and more. Fortunately, treatment programs are also readily available for those who want them. Outpatient methadone programs give heroin addicts the medication methadone to reduce cravings for heroin and block its effects. Patients are also counseled, given vocational guidance and training, and taught how to find support services. Long-term residential programs last for several months to a year. Patients live in a drug-free environment with fellow recovering addicts and counselors. Outpatient drug-free programs use such therapies as problem-solving groups, insight-oriented psychotherapy, cognitive-behavioral therapy, and 12-step programs. Short-term inpatient programs focus on stabilizing the patient, abstinence, and lifestyle changes.

The Job

The main goal of alcohol and drug abuse counselors is to help patients stop their destructive behaviors. Counselors may also work with the families of clients to give them support and guidance in dealing with the problem.

Counselors begin by trying to learn about a patient's general background and history of drug or alcohol use. They may review patient records, including police reports, employment records, medical records, or reports from other counselors.

Counselors also interview the patient to determine the nature and extent of substance abuse. During an interview, the counselor asks questions about what types of substances the patient uses, how often, and for how long. The counselor may also ask patients about previous attempts to stop using the substance and about how the problem has affected their lives in various respects.

Using the information they obtain from the patient and their knowledge of substance abuse patterns, counselors formulate a program for treatment and rehabilitation. A substantial part of the rehabilitation process involves individual, group, or family counseling sessions. During individual sessions, counselors do a great deal of listening, perhaps asking appropriate questions to guide patients to insights about themselves. In group therapy sessions, counselors supervise groups of several patients, helping move their discussion in positive ways. In counseling sessions, counselors also teach patients methods of overcoming their dependencies. For example, they might help a patient develop a series of goals for behavioral change.

Counselors monitor and assess the progress of their patients. In most cases, counselors deal with several different patients in various stages of recovery—some may need help breaking the pattern of substance abuse; some have stopped using, but still need support; others may be recovered users who have suffered a relapse. Counselors maintain ongoing relationships with patients to help them adapt to the different recovery stages.

Working with families is another aspect of many alcohol and drug abuse counselors' jobs. They may ask a patient's family for insight into the patient's behavior. They may also teach the patient's family members how to deal with and support the patient through the recovery process.

Counselors may work with other health professionals and social agencies, including physicians, psychiatrists, psychologists, employment services, and court systems. In some cases, the counselor, with the patient's permission, may serve as a spokesperson for the patient, working with corrections officers, social workers, or employers. In other cases, a patient's needs might exceed the counselor's abilities; when this is the case, the counselor refers the patient to an appropriate medical expert, agency, or social program.

There is a substantial amount of paperwork involved in counseling alcohol and drug abusers. Detailed records must be kept on patients in order to follow their progress. For example, a report must be written after each counseling session. Counselors who work in residential treatment settings are required to participate in regular staff meetings to develop treatment plans and review patient progress. They may also meet periodically with family members or social service agency representatives to discuss patient progress and needs.

In some cases, alcohol and drug abuse counselors specialize in working with certain groups of people. Some work only with children or teenagers; others work with businesses to counsel employees who may have problems related to drugs and alcohol. In still other cases, counselors specialize in treating people who are addicted to specific drugs, such as cocaine, heroin, or alcohol. Counselors may need special training in order to work with specific groups.

Requirements

High School

High school students who are considering a career in alcohol and drug abuse counseling should choose a curriculum that meets the requirements of the college or university they hope to attend. Typically, four years of English, history, mathematics, a foreign language, and social sciences are necessary. In addition, psychology, sociology, physiology, biology, and anatomy provide a good academic background for potential counselors.

The educational requirements for alcohol and drug abuse counselors vary greatly by state and employer. A high school education may be the minimum requirement for employers who provide on-the-job training, which ranges from six weeks to two years. These jobs, however, are becoming increasingly rare as more states are leaning toward stricter requirements for counselors.

Postsecondary Training

Some employers require an associate's degree in alcohol and drug technology. Most substance abuse counselors, however, have a bachelor's degree in counseling, psychology, health sociology, or social work. Many two- and four-year colleges now offer specific courses for students training to be substance abuse counselors.

Many counselors have a master's degree in counseling with a specialization in substance abuse counseling. Accredited graduate programs in substance abuse counseling are composed of a supervised internship as well as regular class work.

Certification or Licensing

Certification in this field, which is mandatory in some states, is available through state accreditation boards. Currently, 39 states and the District of Columbia have credentialing laws for alcohol and drug abuse counselors.

These laws typically require that counselors have a minimum of a master's degree and two to three years of postacademic supervised counseling experience. Candidates must also have passed a written test.

The National Association of Alcoholism and Drug Abuse Counselors also offers a National Certified Addiction Counselor Certification.

Other Requirements

In order to be successful in this job, prospective counselors should enjoy working with people. They must have compassion, good communication and listening skills, and a desire to help others. They should also be emotionally stable and able to deal with the frustrations and failures that are often a part of the job.

Exploring

Students interested in this career can find a great deal of information on substance abuse and substance abuse counseling at any local library. In addition, by contacting a local hospital, mental health clinic, or treatment center, it might be possible to talk with a counselor about the details of his or her job.

Volunteer work or a part-time job at a residential facility, such as a hospital or treatment center, is another good way of gaining experience and exploring an aptitude for counseling work. Finally, the professional and government organizations listed at the end of this article can provide information on alcohol and drug abuse counseling.

Employers

Counselors are hired by hospitals, private and public treatment centers, government agencies, prisons, public school systems, colleges and universities, health maintenance organizations (HMOs), crisis centers, and mental health centers. More and more frequently, large companies are hiring alcohol and drug abuse counselors as well, to deal with employee substance abuse problems.

Starting Out

Counselors who have completed a two- or four-year college degree might start a job search by checking with the career placement office of their college or university. Those who plan to look for a position without first attending college might want to start by getting an entry-level or volunteer position in a treatment center or related agency. In this way, they can obtain practical experience and also make connections that might lead to full-time employment as a counselor.

Job seekers should also watch the classified advertisements in local newspapers. Job openings for counselors are often listed under "Alcohol and Drug Counselor," "Substance Abuse Counselor," or "Mental Health Counselor." Finally, one might consider applying directly to the personnel department of various facilities and agencies that treat alcohol and drug abusers.

Advancement

Counselors in this field often advance initially by taking on more responsibilities and earning a higher wage. They may also better themselves by taking a similar position in a more prestigious facility, such as an upscale private treatment center.

As they obtain more experience and perhaps more education, counselors sometimes move into supervisory or administrative positions. They might become directors of substance abuse programs in mental health facilities or executive directors of agencies or clinics.

Career options are more diverse for those counselors who continue their education. They may move into research, consulting, or teaching at the college level.

Earnings

Salaries of alcohol and drug abuse counselors depend upon education level, amount of experience, and place of employment. Generally, the more education and experience a counselor has, the higher his or her earnings will be.

Counselors who work in private treatment centers also tend to earn more than their public sector counterparts.

According to a 1997 salary study conducted by the Economic Research Institute, substance abuse counselors with less than five years' experience earned an average of $27,336 a year. Counselors with five to 10 years' experience earned an average of $33,740 a year; those with 10 or more years' experience earned from $38,807 to $48,742 annually. Directors of treatment programs or centers could earn considerably more. Almost all treatment centers provide employee benefits to their full-time counselors. Benefits usually include paid vacations and sick days, insurance, and pension plans.

Work Environment

The hours that an alcohol and drug abuse counselor works depends upon where he or she is employed. Many residential treatment facilities and mental health centers—and all crisis centers—have counselors on duty during evening and weekend hours. Other employers, such as government agencies and universities, are likely to have more conventional working hours.

Work settings for counselors also vary by employer. Counselors may work in private offices, in the rooms or homes of patients, in classrooms, or in meeting rooms. In some cases, they conduct support group sessions in churches, community centers, or schools. For the most part, however, counselors work at the same work site or sites on a daily basis.

The bulk of a counselor's day is spent dealing with various people—patients, families, social workers, and health care professionals. There may be very little time during a workday for quiet reflection or organization.

Working with alcohol and drug abusers can be an emotionally draining experience. Overcoming addiction is a very hard battle, and patients respond to it in various ways. They may be resentful, angry, discouraged, or profoundly depressed. They may talk candidly with their counselors about tragic and upsetting events in their lives. Counselors spend much of their time listening to and dealing with very strong, usually negative, emotions.

This work can also be discouraging, due to a high failure rate. Many alcoholics and drug addicts do not respond to treatment and return immediately to their addictions. Even after months and sometimes years of recovery, many substance abusers suffer relapses. The counselor must learn to cope with the frustration of having his or her patients fail, perhaps repeatedly.

There is a very positive side to drug and alcohol abuse counseling, however. When it is successful, counselors have the satisfaction of knowing that they had a positive effect on someone's life. They have the reward of seeing some patients return to happy family lives and productive careers.

Outlook

Employment of alcohol and drug abuse counselors is projected to grow much faster than the average for all occupations through 2008. There are more than 20 million alcoholics in the United States and an equal, if not greater, number of drug abusers. Because no successful method to significantly reduce drug and alcohol abuse has emerged, these numbers are not likely to decrease. Overall population growth will also lead to a need for more substance abuse counselors.

Another reason for the growth in counselors' jobs is that an increasing number of employers are offering employee assistance programs that provide counseling services for mental health and alcohol and drug abuse.

Finally, many job openings will arise as a result of job turnover. Because of the stress levels and the emotional demands involved in this career, there is a high burnout rate. As alcohol and drug abuse counselors leave the field, new counselors are needed to replace them.

For More Information

For more information on substance abuse and counseling careers, contact the following organizations:

American Counseling Association
5999 Stevenson Avenue
Alexandria, VA 22304-3300
Tel: 800-347-6647
Web: http://www.counseling.org/

National Association of Alcoholism and Drug Abuse Counselors
901 North Washington Street, Suite 600
Alexandria, VA 22314-1535
Tel: 800-548-0497
Web: http://www.naadac.org

National Institute on Alcohol Abuse and Alcoholism
National Institutes of Health
6000 Executive Boulevard
Bethesda, MD 20892-7003
Tel: 301-443-3860
Web: http://www.niaaa.nih.gov/

National Institute on Drug Abuse
National Institutes of Health
6001 Executive Boulevard, Room 5213
Bethesda, MD 20892-9561
Tel: 301-443-1124
Web: http://www.nida.nih.gov

For additional information, check out the following Web site run by the Substance Abuse and Mental Health Services Administration:

Prevline: Prevention Online
Substance Abuse and Mental Health Services Administration
5600 Fishers Lane
Rockville, MD 20857
Tel: 301-443-8956
Email: info@samhsa.gov
Web: http://www.health.org

Career and Employment Counselors and Technicians

	School Subjects
Business	
Psychology	
Sociology	

	Personal Skills
Communication/ideas	
Helping/teaching	

	Work Environment
Primarily indoors	
Primarily one location	

	Minimum Education Level
High school diploma	

	Salary Range
$15,000 to $36,650 to $100,000+	

	Certification or Licensing
Voluntary	

	Outlook
Faster than the average	

Overview

Career and employment counselors and technicians, who are also known as *vocational counselors,* provide advice to individuals or groups about occupations, careers, career decision making, career planning, and other career development related questions or conflicts. *Career guidance technicians* collect pertinent information to support both the counselor and applicant during the job search.

History

The first funded employment office in the United States was established in San Francisco in 1886. However, it wasn't until the turn of the century that public interest in improving educational conditions began to develop. The Civic Service House in Boston began the United States' first program of vocational guidance, and the Vocational Bureau was established in 1908 to help young people choose, train, and enter appropriate careers.

The idea of vocational counseling became so appealing that by 1910 a national conference on vocational guidance was held in Boston. The federal government gave support to vocational counseling by initiating a program to assist veterans of World War I in readjusting to civilian life. During the Depression years, agencies such as the Civilian Conservation Corps and the National Youth Administration made attempts at vocational counseling.

On June 6, 1933, the Wagner-Pyser Act established the United States Employment Service. States came into the Service one by one, with each state developing its own plan under the prescribed limits of the Act. By the end of World War II, the Veterans Administration was counseling more than 50,000 veterans each month. Other state and federal government agencies now involved with vocational guidance services include the Bureau of Indian Affairs, the Bureau of Apprenticeship and Training, the Office of Manpower Development, and the Department of Education. In 1980, the National Career Development Association (NCDA), founded in 1913, established a committee for the pre-service and in-service training of vocational guidance personnel. The NCDA established a national credentialing process in 1984.

The profession of employment counseling has become important to the welfare of society as well as to the individuals within it. Each year thousands of people need help in acquiring the kinds of information that make it possible for them to take advantage of today's career opportunities.

The Job

Certified career counselors help people make decisions and plan life and career directions. They tailor strategies and techniques to the specific needs of the person seeking help. Counselors conduct individual and group counseling sessions to help identify life and career goals. They administer and interpret tests and inventories to assess abilities and interests and identify career options. They may use career planning and occupational information to help individuals better understand the work world. They assist in developing individualized career plans, teach job-hunting strategies and skills, and help develop resumes. Sometimes this involves resolving personal conflicts on the job. They also provide support for people experiencing job stress, job loss, and career transition.

Vocational-rehabilitation counselors work with disabled individuals to help the counselees understand what skills they have to offer to an employer. A good counselor knows the working world and how to obtain detailed information about specific jobs. To assist with career decisions, counselors must know about the availability of jobs, the probable future of certain jobs, the education or training necessary to enter them, the kinds of salary or other benefits that certain jobs offer, the conditions that certain jobs impose on employees (night work, travel, work outdoors), and the satisfaction that certain jobs provide their employees. *Professional career counselors* work in both private and public settings and are certified by the National Board for Certified Counselors.

College career planning and placement counselors work exclusively with the students of their universities or colleges. They may specialize in some specific area appropriate to the students and graduates of the school, such as law and education, as well as in part-time and summer work, internships, and field placements. In a liberal arts college, the students may need more assistance in identifying an appropriate career. To do this, the counselor administers interest and aptitude tests and interviews students to determine their career goals.

The counselor may work with currently enrolled students who are seeking internships and other work programs while still at school. Alumni who wish to make a career change also seek the services of the career counseling and placement office at their former schools.

College placement counselors also gather complete job information from prospective employers, and make the information available to interested students and alumni. Just as counselors try to find applicants for particular job listings, they also must seek out jobs for specific applicants. To do this, they will call potential employers to encourage them to consider a qualified individual.

College and career planning and placement counselors are responsible for the arrangements and details of on-campus interviews by large corporations. They also maintain an up-to-date library of vocational guidance material and recruitment literature.

Counselors also give assistance in preparing the actual job search by helping the applicant to write resumes and letters of application, as well as by practicing interview skills through role playing and other techniques. They also provide information on business procedures and personnel requirements in the applicant's chosen field. At universities with access to the

Internet, counselors will set up online accounts for students, giving them access to information regarding potential employers.

Some career planning and placement counselors work with secondary school authorities, advising them on the needs of local industries and specific preparation requirements for both employment and further education. In two-year colleges the counselor may participate in the planning of course content, and in some smaller schools the counselor may be required to teach as well.

The principal duty of career guidance technicians is to help order, catalog, and file materials relating to job opportunities, careers, technical schools, scholarships, careers in the armed forces, and other programs. Guidance technicians also help students and teachers find materials relating to a student's interests and aptitudes. These various materials may be in the form of books, pamphlets, magazine articles, microfiche, videos, computer software, or other media.

Often, career guidance technicians help students take and score self-administered tests that determine their aptitude and interest in different careers or job-related activities. If the career guidance center has audiovisual equipment, such as VCRs or film or slide projectors, career guidance technicians are usually responsible for the equipment.

Requirements

High School

In order to work in the career and employment counseling field, you must have at least a high school diploma. For most jobs in the field, however, higher education is required. In high school, in addition to studying a core curriculum—courses in English, history, mathematics, and so on—you should take courses in psychology, sociology, and business.

Postsecondary Training

When hiring a career guidance technician, most employers look for applicants who have completed two years of training beyond high school, usually at a junior, community, or technical college. These two-year programs, which usually lead to an associate's degree, may combine classroom instruction with practical or sometimes even on-the-job experience.

In some states the minimum educational program in career and vocational counseling is a graduate degree in counseling or a related field from a regionally accredited higher education institution, and a completed supervised counseling experience, which includes career counseling. A growing number of institutions offer post-master's degrees with training in career development and career counseling. Such programs are highly recommended for people who wish to specialize in vocational and career counseling. These programs are frequently called Advanced Graduate Specialist programs or Certificates of Advanced Study programs.

For a career as a college career planning and placement counselor, the minimum educational requirement is commonly a master's degree in guidance and counseling, education, college student personnel work, behavioral science, or a related field. Graduate work includes courses in vocational and aptitude testing, counseling techniques, personnel management and occupational research, industrial relations, and group dynamics and organizational behavior.

As in any profession, there is usually an initial period of training for newly hired counselors and counselor trainees. Some of the skills needed by employment counselors, such as testing-procedures skills and interviewing skills, can only be acquired through on-the-job training.

Certification or Licensing

The National Board for Certified Counselors offers the National Certified Counselor (NCC) designation. Applicants must have earned a master's degree with a major study in counseling and take and pass the National Counselor Examination. NCCs are certified for a period of five years. In order to be recertified, they must complete 100 contact clock hours of continuing education or pass the examination again.

Other Requirements

A career counselor must have a good background in education, training, employment trends, the current labor market, and career resources. Counselors should be able to provide their clients with information about job tasks, functions, salaries, requirements, and the future outlook of broad occupational fields.

Knowledge of testing techniques and measures of aptitude, achievement, interests, values, and personality is required. The ability to evaluate job performance and individual effectiveness is helpful. The career counselor must also have management and administrative skills.

Exploring

Summer work in an employment agency is a good way to explore the field of employment counseling. Interviewing the director of a public or private agency might give you a better understanding of what the work involves and the qualifications such an organization requires of its counselors.

Interested high school students who enjoy working with others will find helpful experiences in working in the dean's or counselor's office. Many schools offer opportunities in peer tutoring, both in academics and in career guidance-related duties. (If your school does not have such a program in place, consider putting together a proposal to institute one. Your guidance counselor should be able to help you with this.) A student's own experience in seeking summer and part-time work is also valuable in learning what the job seeker must confront in business or industry. You could write a feature story for your school newspaper on your and others' experiences in the working world.

If you are interested in becoming a career counselor, you should seek out professional career counselors and discuss the field with them. Most people are happy to talk about what they do.

High school students interested in becoming career guidance technicians should consider working part-time or as a volunteer in a library. Such work can provide students with some of the basic skills for learning about information resources, cataloging, and filing. In addition, assisting schools or clubs with any media presentations, such as video or slide shows, will help familiarize a student with the equipment used by counselors.

Employers

Career and employment counselors work in guidance offices of high schools, colleges, and universities. They are also employed by state, federal, and other bureaus of employment, and by social service agencies.

Starting Out

Journals specializing in information for career counselors frequently have job listings or information on job hotlines and services. School placement centers also are a good source of information, both because of their standard practice of listing job openings from participating firms and because schools are a likely source of jobs for career counselors. Placement officers will be aware of which schools are looking for applicants.

To enter the field of college career planning and placement, interested alumni may consider working for their alma maters as assistants in the college or university placement office. Other occupational areas that provide an excellent background for college placement work include teaching, business, public relations, previous placement training, positions in employment agencies, and experience in psychological counseling.

Career guidance technicians should receive some form of career placement from schools offering training in that area. Newspapers may list entry-level jobs. One of the best methods, however, is to contact libraries and education centers directly to inquire about their needs for assistance in developing or staffing their career guidance centers.

Advancement

Employment counselors in federal or state employment services or in other vocational counseling agencies are usually considered trainees for the first six months of their employment. During this time, they learn the specific skills that will be expected of them during their careers with these agencies. The first year of a new counselor's employment is probationary.

Positions of further responsibility include supervisory or administrative work, which may be attained by counselors after several years of experience on the job. Advancement to administrative positions often means giving up the actual counseling work, which is not an advantage to those who enjoy working with people in need of counseling.

Opportunity for advancement for college counselors—to assistant and associate placement director, director of student personnel services, or similar administrative positions—depends largely upon the type of college or university and the size of the staff. In general, a doctorate is preferred and may be necessary for advancement.

New employees in agencies are frequently considered trainees for the first six months to a year of their employment. During the training period, they acquire the specific skills that will be required of them during their tenure with the agency. Frequently, the first year of employment is probationary. After several years' experience on the job, counselors may reach supervisory or administrative positions.

Earnings

Salaries vary greatly within the career and vocational counseling field. Median salaries for full-time educational and vocational counselors were $36,650 in 1998, according to the U.S. Department of Labor. The lowest 10 percent earned less than $21,230 and the highest 10 percent earned more than $73,920. Those in business or industry earn somewhat higher salaries.

In private practice, the range is yet wider. Some practitioners earn as little as $20,000 per year and others earn in excess of $100,000 per year.

Annual earnings of career planning and placement counselors vary greatly among educational institutions, with larger institutions offering the highest salaries. Benefits include holidays and vacations, pension and retirement plans, and, in some institutions, reduced tuition.

Salaries for career guidance technicians vary according to education and experience and the geographic location of the job. In general, career guidance technicians who are graduates of two-year post-high school training programs can expect to receive starting salaries averaging $15,000 to $20,000 a year.

Work Environment

Employment counselors usually work about 40 hours a week, but some agencies are more flexible. Counseling is done in offices designed to be free from noise and distractions, to allow confidential discussions with clients.

College career planning and placement counselors also normally work a 40-hour week, although irregular hours and overtime are frequently required during the peak recruiting period. They generally work on a 12-month basis.

Career guidance technicians work in very pleasant surroundings, usually in the career guidance office of a college or vocational school. They will interact with a great number of students, some of whom are eagerly looking for work, others who are more tense and anxious. The technician must remain unruffled in order to ease any tension and provide a quiet atmosphere.

Outlook

There should be faster-than-average growth in the field of employment counseling through 2008, according to the U.S. Department of Labor. Although only moderate opportunities are anticipated for employment and rehabilitation counselors in state and local governments, rapid growth is expected in the development of human resource and employment assistance programs in private business and industry, which should produce more jobs.

Libraries and schools have had increasingly limited budgets for staff and resources. Competition for jobs for career guidance technicians is increasingly stiff. The needs of outplacement centers, employment agencies, and armed forces offices are remaining somewhat stagnant. If there is an increased focus on retraining workers or educating students about career options, there may be an increase in the future demand for career guidance technicians.

For More Information

For a variety of career resources for career seekers and career counseling professionals, contact the following organizations:

American Counseling Association
5999 Stevenson Avenue
Alexandria, VA 22304-3300
Tel: 800-347-6647
Web: http://www.counseling.org/

Career Planning and Adult Development Network
PO Box 1484
Pacifica, CA 94044
Tel: 650-359-6911
Web: http://www.careernetwork.org/

To read the online version of Job Choices, *which provides resume and interview tips, general career information, and advice from the experts, check out NACE's Web site:*

National Association of Colleges and Employers (NACE)
62 Highland Avenue
Bethlehem, PA 18017-9085
Tel: 800-544-5272
Web: http://www.jobweb.org/

For information on certification, contact:

National Board for Certified Counselors
3 Terrace Way, Suite D
Greensboro, NC 27403-3660
Tel: 336-547-0607
Email: nbcc@nbcc.org
Web: http://www.nbcc.org/

For more information on career counselors, contact:

National Career Development Association
10820 East 45th Street, Suite 210
Tulsa, OK 74146
Tel: 918-663-7060
Web: http://ncda.org

Child Life Specialists

Health Psychology	School Subjects
Communication/ideas Helping/teaching	Personal Skills
Primarily indoors Primarily one location	Work Environment
Bachelor's degree	Minimum Education Level
$12,500 to $28,560 to $70,000	Salary Range
Recommended	Certification or Licensing
About as fast as the average	Outlook

Overview

Child life specialists work in health care settings to help infants, children, adolescents, and their families through illness or injury. One of the primary roles of the child life specialist is to ease the anxiety and stress that often accompany hospitalization, injury, or routine medical care. Child life specialists help children, adolescents, and their families maintain living patterns that are as close to normal as possible, and they try to minimize the potential trauma of hospitalization. Specialists do this by providing opportunities for play and relaxation, interaction with other children, and personalized attention. They also encourage family involvement, which can play a major role in helping children and adolescents cope with difficult situations. Child life specialists may help children and their families to develop coping skills and educate them about the experience that they are going through.

Some hospitals refer to their child life specialists as *play therapists, patient activity therapists, activity therapists,* or *therapeutic recreation specialists.*

History

At one time physicians and nurses were the only adults responsible for the care of children in hospitals. Parents left their children in hospitals, frequently for long periods of time, for treatment of their illnesses. But many parents felt that their children's emotional needs were not being met. Children were often not told about what tests, treatments, or procedures they were to undergo, and as a result their hospital experience was frequently traumatic. In addition, social workers who were part of the health care team sometimes were not specially trained to work with children and could not provide them with support.

During the early 20th century attempts were made to improve health care workers' understanding of children's needs and to make hospital stays less emotionally difficult for children. C. S. Mott Hospital in Ann Arbor, Michigan, for example, created the nation's first child life department, focusing on child development, in 1922. Gradually, during the 1940s and 1950s, "play programs" were developed at various care facilities across the country. In these settings children were allowed to relax, play, and feel safe. As professional interest in and understanding of child development grew, the play programs began to be seen not only as a playtime but also as a therapeutic part of children's care during hospital stays. During the 1960s and 1970s the field of child life grew dramatically as it gained increasing acceptance.

The profession of child life specialists was formally recognized in 1974, when the Association for the Care of Children's Health formed a committee for child life and activity specialists. The committee, which became the independent organization Child Life Council in 1982, had as its goals to promote the profession of child life specialist as well as to strengthen these specialists' professional identity. The committee's members recognized that the interruption of a hospitalization or even an ambulatory procedure can have negative consequences for children's growth and development. Today, child life specialists are recognized as an integral part of a child's health care team.

The Job

When children are hospitalized, the experience can be frightening. Child life specialists need to be tuned into the child's or adolescent's concerns. For some children, separation from their families and the familiarity of home can be traumatic. For others, repeated blood tests, needles, or painful procedures can cause fears or nightmares. Emotional damage can be a danger even for adolescents. No matter how short or long the hospital stay and no matter how serious the illness or injury, children can experience anxiety or other emotional effects.

Child life specialists try to ease the possible trauma of being in the hospital. They play an important role in educating and comforting both the patients and their families. They become familiar and trusted adults, and they are usually the only professionals who do not perform tests on the children.

Child life specialists may use dolls and medical instruments to show children what the doctor will be doing. They may help children act out their concerns by having them give a doll a shot if they receive one. The child life specialist may use recreational activities, art projects, cooking, music, and outdoor play in their work. Programs are tailored to meet the needs of individual patients. Some children are unable to express their fears and concerns and may need the child life specialist to draw them out. Some children rely on the child life specialist to help them understand what is happening to them. Still others need the child life specialist to explain children's emotional outbursts or withdrawal to their families.

When children are hospitalized for a long period of time, child life specialists may accompany them to procedures, celebrate successful treatment, or plan a holiday celebration. Specialists may also take children on preadmission orientation and hospital tours. They serve as advocates for children's issues by promoting rooming-in or unrestricted parental or sibling visits. Many child life specialists work in conjunction with local school districts to help children keep up with school while they are in the hospital.

Child life administrators supervise the staffs of child life personnel. In larger hospitals, the administrators work with other hospital administrators to run the child life programs smoothly within the hospital setting.

Child life specialists can turn their patients' hospital stays into a time of growth. Children are very resilient, and with proper care by their entire health team, they can emerge from hospital stays with a sense of accomplishment and heightened self-esteem.

Requirements

High School

If you are interested in becoming a child life specialist, you will need to plan on going to college after high school. Therefore, you should take a college preparatory curriculum. As a child life specialist you will need to understand family dynamics, child development, educational play, and basic medical terminology. To help you prepare for this speciality, take psychology and sociology courses and, if available, child development classes. In addition, be sure that your class schedule includes science courses, including health and biology. Because communication is such an important aspect of this work, take English, communication, and speech classes. You may also want to take art, physical education, and drama classes to develop skills that you can use in a variety of therapies, such as play, art, and recreation therapy.

Postsecondary Training

Some colleges or universities offer specific programs in child life, and quite a number of schools offer course work in areas related to child life. Those who attend colleges or universities that do not have specific child life programs should major in another appropriate field, such as child development, psychology, and social work. Do some research before you select a school to attend. The Child Life Council (CLC) advises those considering this career to look for a school program that has sufficient faculty, a variety of field opportunities, and positive student evaluations. The CLC offers the *Directory of Child Life Programs,* which has information on both undergraduate and graduate programs. Typical classes to take include child psychology, child growth and development, family dynamics, and theories of play. Select a program that offers internships. An internship will give you supervised experience in the field as well as prepare you for future employment.

A child life administrator is usually required to have a master's degree in child development, behavioral psychology, education, or a related field. Graduate level course work typically includes the areas of administration, research, and advanced clinical issues. Those who wish to be considered for positions as child life administrators must also have work experience supervising staff members, managing budgets, and preparing educational materials.

Certification or Licensing

Certification as a Certified Child Life Specialist is available through the CLC. Certification criteria include passing an examination and fulfilling education requirements. Although certification is voluntary, it is highly recommended. Some health care centers will not hire a child life specialist who is not certified.

Other Requirements

To be a successful child life specialist you should enjoy working with people, especially children. You will be part of a health care team, so you must be able to communicate effectively with medical professionals as well as able to communicate with children and their families. You must be creative in order to come up with different ways to explain complicated events, such as a surgery, to a child without frightening him or her. You will also need maturity and emotional stability to deal with situations that may otherwise upset you, such as seeing chronically ill or severely injured children. Those who enjoy this work are able to focus on its positive aspects—helping children and their families through difficult times.

Exploring

An excellent way to explore your interest in and aptitude for this work is to volunteer. For volunteer opportunities in medical settings, find out what local hospitals, out-patient clinics, or nursing homes have to offer. Opportunities to work with children are also available through organizations such as Easter Seals, Boy Scouts and Girl Scouts, and Big Brothers/Big Sisters of America. In addition, volunteer or paid positions are available at many summer camps. Baby-sitting, of course, is another way to work with children as well as earn extra money. And a good baby-sitter is always in demand, no matter where you live.

Once you are in college you can join CLC as a student member. Membership includes a subscription to the council's newsletter, which can give you a better understanding of the work of a child life specialist.

Employers

Child life specialists work as members of the health care team typically in hospitals. Increasingly, though, child life specialists are finding employment outside of hospitals at such places as rehabilitation centers, hospices, and ambulatory care facilities. Most child life programs in hospitals are autonomous and report to hospital administrations in the same manner as other departments and programs.

Child life programs often work with school programs within hospitals. Specialists may work with teachers to coordinate the curriculum with recreational activities. They also may encourage hospital administrations to provide adequate classroom facilities and highly qualified teachers.

Starting Out

Your internship may provide you with valuable contacts that can give you information on job leads. In addition, the career center or placement office of your college or university should be able to help you locate your first job. The Child Life Council offers its members use of a job bank that lists openings at hospitals and clinics. You may also contact hospitals' placement offices directly for information on available positions.

Advancement

Becoming certified and keeping up with new developments through continuing education workshops and seminars are the first two steps anyone must take in order to advance in this field. The next step is to get a graduate degree. Advancement possibilities include the positions of child life administrator, assistant director, or director of a child life program. Advanced positions involve management responsibilities including the overseeing of a staff and coordinating a program's activities. Those in advanced positions must also keep their knowledge up to date by completing continuing education, attending professional conferences, and reading professional journals.

Earnings

Salaries for child life specialists vary greatly depending on such factors as the region of the country a specialist works in, education level, certification, and the size of the employer. For example, salaries tend to be higher in large metropolitan teaching hospitals than in small community hospitals. In 2000, the Department of Human Development and Family Studies of the University of Alabama, Tuscaloosa, conducted a salary survey of child life professionals to determine national salary trends for the field. According to this survey, those just starting out in the field had annual salaries ranging from a low of $12,500 to a high of approximately $55,540. The mean income for this group was approximately $28,560. Those with three to five years of work experience had mean annual earnings of $31,585. Child life specialists with more than 10 years of experience reported salaries ranging from $30,000 to $70,000 annually, with a mean income of approximately $40,920. Those with the highest earnings are usually child life administrators or directors. In addition, those with certification tend to earn more than their noncertified counterparts.

Benefits vary by employer, but they usually include such items as paid vacation and sick days, medical insurance, and retirement plans.

Work Environment

Child life specialists are members of the health care team in a variety of settings, including hospitals, clinics, and hospice facilities. In most hospitals, the child life specialist works in a special playroom. Sometimes the specialist may go to the child's hospital room. In outpatient facilities, the specialist may work in a waiting room or a designated playroom. According to the American Academy of Pediatrics, the ratio of child life specialists to children that works well is about one to 15. Child life specialists must be comfortable in hospital settings. They need to adjust easily to being around children who are sick. Since the children and their families need so much support, child life specialists need to be emotionally stable. Their own support network of family and friends should be strong, so that the specialist can get through difficult times at work. Child life specialists may have patients who die, and this can be difficult.

Most child life personnel work during regular business hours, although specialists are occasionally needed on evenings, holidays, or weekends to work with the children. It is important for child life personnel to have hobbies or outside interests to avoid becoming too emotionally drained from the work. The rewards of a child life career are great. Many child life specialists see the direct effects of their work on their patients and on their patients' families. They see anxiety and fear being eased, and they see their patients come through treatments and hospitalizations with a renewed pride.

Outlook

The employment outlook for child life specialists is good. The American Academy of Pediatrics reports that most hospitals specializing in pediatric care have child life programs. In addition, the number of these programs has doubled since 1965. And although managed-care providers encourage short hospital stays that may result in a reduced need for staffing in hospitals, opportunities for child life specialists are increasing outside of the hospital setting. The possible employers of today and tomorrow include outpatient clinics, rehabilitation centers, hospice programs, and other facilities that may treat children, such as sexual assault centers and centers for abused women and children.

For More Information

For current news on issues affecting children's health, contact:

American Academy of Pediatrics
141 Northwest Point Boulevard
Elk Grove Village, IL 60007-1098
Tel: 847-434-4000
Web: http://www.aap.org

For education, career, and certification information as well as professional publications, contact:

Child Life Council
11820 Parklawn Drive, Suite 202
Rockville, MD 20852-2529
Tel: 301-881-7090
Email: clcstaff@childlife.org
Web: http://www.childlife.org

For information on children's health issues and pediatric care, contact:

National Association of Children's Hospitals and Related Institutions
401 Wythe Street
Alexandria, VA 22314
Tel: 703-684-1355
Web: http://www.childrenshospitals.net/nachri

Creative Arts Therapists

Art Music Theater/dance	School Subjects
Artistic Helping/teaching	Personal Skills
Master's degree	Minimum Education Level
$16,380 to $27,760 to $62,120	Salary Range
Required by all states	Certification or Licensing
About as fast as the average	Outlook

Overview

Creative arts therapists treat and rehabilitate people with mental, physical, and emotional disabilities. They use the creative processes of music, art, dance/movement, drama, psychodrama, and poetry in their therapy sessions to determine the underlying causes of some problems and to help patients achieve therapeutic goals. Creative arts therapists usually specialize in one particular type of therapeutic activity. The specific objectives of the therapeutic activities vary according to the needs of the patient and the setting of the therapy program.

History

Creative arts therapy programs are fairly recent additions to the health care field. Although many theories of mental and physical therapy have existed for centuries, it has been only in the last 70 years or so that health care professionals have truly realized the healing powers of music, art, dance, and other forms of artistic self-expression.

Art therapy is based on the idea that people who can't discuss their problems with words must have another outlet for self-expression. In the early 1900s, psychiatrists began to look more closely at their patients' artwork, realizing that there could be links between the emotional or psychological illness and the art. Sigmund Freud even did some preliminary research into the artistic expression of his patients.

In the 1930s, art educators discovered that children often expressed their thoughts better with pictures and role-playing than they did through verbalization. Children often don't know the words they need to explain how they feel, or how to make their needs known to adults. Researchers began to look into art as a way to treat children who were traumatized by abuse, neglect, illness, or other physical or emotional disabilities.

During and after World War II, the Department of Veterans Affairs (VA) developed and organized various art, music, and dance activities for patients in VA hospitals. These activities had a dramatic effect on the physical and mental well being of the World War II veterans, and creative arts therapists began to help treat and rehabilitate patients in other health care settings.

Because of early breakthroughs with children and veterans, the number of arts therapists has increased greatly over the past few decades, and the field has expanded to include drama, psychodrama, and poetry, as well as the more traditional music, art, and dance. Today creative arts therapists work with diverse populations of patients in a wide range of facilities, and they focus on the specific needs of a vast spectrum of disorders and disabilities. Colleges and universities offer degree programs in many types of therapies, and national associations for registering and certifying creative arts therapists work to monitor training programs and to ensure the professional integrity of the therapists working in the various fields.

The Job

Similar to dreaming, creative arts therapy taps into the subconscious and gives people a mode of expression in an uncensored environment. This is important because before patients can begin to heal, they must first identify their feelings. Once they recognize their feelings, they can begin to develop an understanding of the relationship between their feelings and their behavior.

The main goal of a creative arts therapist is to improve the patient's physical, mental, and emotional health. Before they begin any treatment, they meet with a team of other health care professionals. After determining the strength, limitations, and interests of their patient, they create a program to promote positive change and growth in the patient. The creative arts therapist continues to confer with the other health care workers as the program progresses, and alters the program according to the patient's progress. How these goals are reached depends on the unique specialty of the therapist in question.

"It's like sitting in the woods waiting for a fawn to come out." That is how Barbara Fish, director of activity therapy for the Illinois Department of Mental Health and Developmental Disabilities, describes her experience as she waits patiently for a sexually abused patient to begin to trust her. The patient is extraordinarily frightened because of the traumatic abuse she has suffered. This may be the first time in the patient's life that she is in an environment of acceptance and support. It may take months or even years before the patient begins to trust the therapist, "come out of the woods," and begin to heal.

In some cases, especially when the patients are adolescents, they may have become so detached from their feelings that they can physically act out without consciously knowing the reasons for their behavior. This detachment from their emotions creates a great deal of psychological pain. With the help of a creative arts therapist, patients can begin to communicate their subconscious feelings both verbally and nonverbally. They can express their emotions in a variety of ways without having to name them.

Creative arts therapists work with all age groups: young children, adolescents, adults, and senior citizens. They can work in individual, group, or family sessions. The approach of the therapist, however, depends on the specific needs of the patient or group. For example, if a patient is feeling overwhelmed by too many options or stimuli, the therapist may give him or her only a plain piece of paper and a pencil to work with that day.

Barbara Fish has three ground rules for her art therapy sessions with disturbed adolescents: respect yourself, respect other people, and respect property. The therapy groups are limited to five patients per group. She begins the session by asking each person in the group how he or she is feeling that day. By carefully listening to their responses, a theme may emerge that will determine the direction of the therapy. For example, if anger is reoccurring in their statements, Fish may ask them to draw a line down the center of a piece of paper. On one side, she will ask them to draw how anger looks and on the other side how feeling sad looks. Then, once the drawing is complete, she will ask them to compare the two pictures and see that their anger may be masking their feelings of sadness, loneliness, and disappointment. As patients begin to recognize their true feelings, they develop better control of their behavior.

To reach their patients, creative arts therapists can use a variety of mediums, including visual art, music, dance, drama, or poetry or other kinds of creative writing. Creative arts therapists usually specialize in a specific medium, becoming a music therapist, drama therapist, dance therapist, art therapist, or poetry therapist. "In my groups we use poetry and creative writing," Fish explains. "We do all kinds of things to get at what is going on at an unconscious level."

Music therapists use musical lessons and activities to improve a patient's self-confidence and self-awareness, to relieve states of depression, and to improve physical dexterity. For example, a music therapist treating a patient with Alzheimer's might play songs from the patient's past in order to stimulate long- and short-term memory, soothe feelings of agitation, and increase a sense of reality.

Art therapists use art in much the same manner. The art therapist may encourage and teach patients to express their thoughts, feelings, and anxieties via sketching, drawing, painting, or sculpting. Art therapy is especially helpful in revealing patterns of domestic abuse in families. Children involved in such a situation may depict scenes of family life with violent details or portray a certain family member as especially frightening or threatening.

Dance/movement therapists develop and conduct dance/movement sessions to help improve the physical, mental, and emotional health of their patients. Dance and movement therapy is also used as a way of assessing a patient's progress toward reaching therapeutic goals.

There are other types of creative arts therapists as well. *Drama therapists* use role-playing, pantomime (the telling of a story by the use of expressive body or facial movements), puppetry, improvisation, and original scripted dramatization to evaluate and treat patients. *Poetry therapists* and *bibliotherapists*, use the written and spoken word to treat patients.

Requirements

High School

A high school diploma or GED equivalent is mandatory to become a creative arts therapist. Depending on what type of creative arts therapy you might wish to pursue, you should become as proficient as possible with the methods and tools of the trade. For example, if you want to become involved in music therapy, you need to become familiar with musical instruments as well as music theory. A good starting point for a music therapist is to study piano or guitar. It is important that high school students wishing to become creative arts therapists begin studying any applicable art forms as soon as possible. When therapists work with patients they must be able to concentrate completely on the patient rather than on learning how to use tools or techniques.

In addition to courses such as drama, art, music, and English, students should consider taking an introductory class in psychology. Also, students should take a communication class to begin to gain an understanding of the various ways people communicate, both verbally and nonverbally.

Postsecondary Training

To become a creative arts therapist one must have earned at least a bachelor's degree, usually in the area in which one wishes to specialize. However, to be accredited, many nationally recognized associations require a graduate degree from a university with an accredited program. For instance, the American Association for Art Therapy requires a master's degree for accreditation.

Accredited graduate programs for creative arts therapists vary according to the discipline pursued. For example, graduate programs in art therapy require the applicant to submit a portfolio of original artwork. The portfolio should demonstrate a high level of competence with working with art materials, although not necessarily a great degree of talent.

Once accepted into a program, art therapy students undergo rigorous classroom instruction that includes at least 15 semester hours of study in studio art and 12 semester hours of psychology. It is a requirement that these hours of study be completed within a year of beginning the program. In addition to class work, students must participate in 600 hours of supervised arts therapy practice, half of which is in individual sessions and half in group sessions. Finally, the core curriculum includes 21 graduate credit hours, which the student must complete within two years or four full-time semesters. Requirements in graduate programs for most of the other areas of creative arts therapy are similar to those for art therapists.

Certification or Licensing

The nationally recognized association specific to their field of choice must certify most creative arts therapists. For instance, certification by the Art Therapy Credentials Board, Inc. (ATCB) is a two-part process. First, to become registered, the ATCB will review the applicant's documentation of graduate education and postgraduate supervised experience. Once the arts therapist is registered, he or she must pass a written examination administered by the ATCB to become board certified. To retain this status, therapists must continue their education.

Certification for most other creative arts therapies also requires passing a national examination. For example, a music therapist must pass an exam administered by the Certification Board for Music Therapists. The examination tests competence in individual skills and knowledge, and the practical application of professional music therapy.

Many registered creative arts therapists also receive additional licenses as social workers, educators, mental health professionals, or marriage and family therapists. They are also often members of other professional associations, including the American Psychological Association, the American Association of Marriage and Family Therapists, and the American Counseling Association.

Other Requirements

Creative arts therapists should have a strong desire to help others seek positive change in their lives. All types of creative arts therapists must be able to work well with other people—both patients and other health professionals—in the development and implementation of therapy programs. They must have the patience and the stamina to teach and practice therapy with patients for whom progress is often very slow because of their various physical and emotional disorders. A therapist must always keep in mind that even a tiny amount of progress might be extremely significant for some patients and their families. A good sense of humor is also a valuable trait for someone working in the field.

Exploring

There are many ways to explore the possibility of a career as a creative arts therapist. Students can write to professional associations for information on therapy careers. They can talk with people working in the creative arts therapy field and perhaps arrange to observe a creative arts therapy session. To see if they would be happy working in the field, students may seek part-time or summer jobs or volunteer at a hospital, clinic, nursing home, or any of a number of health care facilities.

A summer job as an aide at a camp for disabled children, for example, may help provide insight into the nature of creative arts therapy, including both its rewards and demands. Such experience can be very valuable in deciding if you are suited to the inherent frustrations of a therapy career.

Employers

Creative arts therapists usually work as members of an interdisciplinary health care team that may include physicians, nurses, social workers, psychiatrists, and psychologists. Although often employed in hospitals, therapists also work in rehabilitation centers, nursing homes, day treatment facilities, shelters for battered women, pain and stress management clinics, substance abuse programs, hospices, and correctional facilities. Others maintain their own private practices. Many creative arts therapists work with children in grammar and high schools, either as therapists or art teachers. Some arts therapists teach or conduct research in the creative arts at colleges and universities.

Starting Out

After earning a bachelor's degree in a particular field, potential creative arts therapists should complete their certification, which may include an internship or assistantship. Unpaid training internships often can lead to a first job in the field. Graduates can utilize the placement office at their college or university to help them find positions in the creative arts therapy field. Many professional associations also compile lists of job openings to assist their members.

Creative arts therapists who are new to the field might consider doing volunteer work at a nonprofit community organization, correctional facility, or other neighborhood association to gain some practical experience. Therapists who want to start their own practice can host group therapy sessions in their home. Creative arts therapists may also wish to associate themselves with other members of the alternative health care field in order to gain experience and build a client base.

Advancement

As therapists gain more experience, they can move into supervisory, administrative, or teaching positions. Often, the supervision of interns can resemble a therapy session. The interns will discuss their feelings and ask any questions that they may have regarding their work with patients. How did they handle their patients? What were the reactions to what their patients said or did? What could they be doing to help their patients more? The *supervising therapist* helps the interns become competent creative arts therapists.

Many therapists have represented the profession internationally. Barbara Fish was invited to present her paper, "Art Therapy with Children and Adolescents," at the University of Helsinki. Additionally, Fish spoke in Finland at a three-day workshop exploring the use and effectiveness of arts therapy with children and adolescents. Raising the public and professional awareness of creative arts therapy is an important concern for many therapists.

Earnings

Because creative arts therapies are very broad in nature and are often used in conjunction with other treatments, it is difficult to estimate exact salary ranges for each subset (music therapists, drama therapists, etc.). As noted in the *Occupational Outlook Handbook,* the median annual earnings of recreational therapists (who have many of the same duties and qualifications as creative arts therapists) were about $27,760 in 1998. Most earn between $21,580 and $35,000 a year, although salaries can range from less than $16,380 to $42,440 a year.

Creative arts therapists who run their own practices may earn less because they have to cover their own business upkeep costs, in addition to advertising and insurance. Professional therapists who use arts therapy in conjunction with other specialties, such as psychiatry and psychology, may earn considerably more. Depending on their education, training, and specialty, psychologists earned between $19,500 and $62,120 in 1997, and creative arts therapists who complete their education in psychology can expect a salary in that range.

Work Environment

Most creative arts therapists work a typical 40-hour, five-day workweek; at times, however, they may have to work extra hours. The number of patients under a therapist's care depends on the specific employment setting. Although many therapists work in hospitals, they may also be employed in such facilities as clinics, rehabilitation centers, children's homes, schools, and nursing homes. Some therapists maintain service contracts with several facilities. For instance, a therapist might work two days a week at a hospital, one day at a nursing home, and the rest of the week at a rehabilitation center.

Most buildings are pleasant, comfortable, and clean places in which to work. Experienced creative arts therapists might choose to be self-employed, working with patients in their own studios. In such a case, the therapist might work more irregular hours to accommodate patient schedules. Other therapists might maintain a combination of service contract work with one or more facilities in addition to a private caseload of clients referred to them by other health care professionals. Whether therapists work on service contracts with various facilities or maintain private practices, they must deal with all of the business and administrative details and worries that go along with being self-employed.

Outlook

The creative arts therapy professions are growing very rapidly, and many new positions are created each year. Although enrollment in college therapy programs is increasing, new graduates are usually able to find jobs. In cases where an individual is unable to find a full-time position, a therapist might obtain service contracts for part-time work at several facilities.

The U.S. Department of Labor predicts that employment of recreational therapists should grow as fast as the average through 2008, because of expansion in long-term care, physical and psychiatric rehabilitation, and services for people with disabilities. Because the occupation is small, the total number of job openings will be relatively low.

Job openings in facilities such as nursing homes should continue to increase as the elderly population grows over the next few decades. Advances in medical technology and the recent practice of early discharge from hospitals should also create new opportunities in managed care facilities, chronic pain clinics, and cancer care facilities. The demand for therapists of all types should continue to increase as more people become aware of the need to help disabled patients in creative ways. Some drama therapists and psychodramatists are also finding employment opportunities outside of the usual health care field. Such therapists might conduct therapy sessions at corporate sites to enhance the personal effectiveness and growth of employees.

For More Information

For more information about various types of art therapy, contact:

National Coalition of Arts Therapies Associations
8455 Colesville Road, Suite 1000
Silver Spring, MD 20910
Tel: 714-751-0103
Web: http://www.ncata.com/

For more detailed information about your field of interest, contact the following organizations:

American Art Therapy Association
1202 Allanson Road
Mundelein, IL 60060-3808
Tel: 847-949-6064
Email: arttherapy@ntr.net
Web: http://www.arttherapy.org

American Dance Therapy Association
2000 Century Plaza, Suite 108
10632 Little Patuxent Parkway
Columbia, MD 21044
Tel: 410-997-4040
Email: info@adta.org
Web: http://www.adta.org/

American Music Therapy Association
8455 Colesville Road, Suite 1000
Silver Spring, MD 20910
Tel: 301-589-3300
Email: info@musictherapy.org
Web: http://www.musictherapy.org/

American Society of Group Psychotherapy and Psychodrama
301 North Harrison Street, Suite 508
Princeton, NJ 08540
Tel: 609-452-1339
Email: asgpp@asgpp.org
Web: http://www.asgpp.org/

National Association for Drama Therapy
5505 Connecticut Avenue, NW, #280
Washington, DC 20015
Tel: 202-966-7409
Web: http://www.nadt.org

National Association for Poetry Therapy
5505 Connecticut Avenue, NW, #280
Washington, DC 20015
Tel: 202-966-2536
Web: http://www.poetrytherapy.org

Geriatric Social Workers

School Subjects	Psychology Sociology
Personal Skills	Helping/teaching Leadership/management
Work Environment	Primarily indoors Primarily multiple locations
Minimum Education Level	Bachelor's degree
Salary Range	$24,000 to $34,250 to $58,880
Certification or Licensing	Recommended (certification) Required by all states (licensing)
Outlook	Faster than the average

Overview

Geriatric social workers, also known as *gerontology social workers,* help elderly people adjust to the challenges of growing older. They develop programs and direct agencies that offer counseling, advocacy, and special services. They evaluate the needs of clients and help them arrange for such things as meal service, housing, transportation, and legal and medical assistance. Geriatric social workers also develop recreation and educational programs for the elderly.

Approximately one-third of all social workers work with older people. They work in hospitals, nursing homes, and retirement communities; they have offices in human service agencies and senior centers. Geriatric social workers must have a genuine interest in the well-being of older people and must be sensitive to their concerns and problems.

The Job

A woman in her late 70s has just lost her husband and now must live alone for the first time in many years. She has decided to move to another town, to live closer to her children, and will need help making the transition. She needs a smaller, more manageable home; she needs help with meals and shopping; she would like to make friends in the community. A number of services are available to her, but she may not find out about them without the aid of a geriatric social worker.

As with any social worker, the geriatric social worker is devoted to helping people and communities solve problems. Social workers are dedicated to empowering people and helping people to preserve their dignity and feeling of worth. This kind of assistance and advocacy is especially important among older people. Because old age can sometimes put a person in poor physical and mental health as well as cause financial difficulties, older people often need help and protection. They may need help with preparing meals, finding transportation, and doing housework, or they may need assistance moving into a retirement community or nursing home. But the elderly population of any community is diverse; some older people stay in perfectly good health, and they rely on social services for recreation, meeting people, educational programs, and grief and loss counseling.

People are living longer these days, and the elderly population is growing. At the beginning of the 20th century, only one-half of newborns would live past the age of 50; people born at the beginning of the 21st century can, on average, expect to live well past the age of 75. This is why social work will continue to offer many job opportunities.

The social work profession is divided into two areas: direct practice and indirect practice. Direct practice is also known as clinical practice. As the name suggests, direct practice involves working directly with the client by offering counseling, advocacy, information and referral, and education. Indirect practice concerns the structures through which the direct practice is offered. Indirect practice (a practice consisting mostly of social workers who hold Ph.D.s) involves program development and evaluation, administration, and policy analysis. Geriatric social workers may work directly with the elderly population through counseling, advising, and conducting group sessions. They also help clients find services for health, housing, finances, and transportation. Those social workers involved in indirect practice develop and oversee the agencies and departments that provide these social services.

Geriatric social workers work for service agencies, hospitals, nursing homes, senior centers, and for other community organizations. Some also work independently. Their help is needed in every town and city across the country; some social workers in areas with smaller populations may serve a number of small towns within a region. No matter where a geriatric social worker serves, the nature of the work is usually the same. Geriatric social workers will meet with older people individually to determine their needs. Home meal delivery programs, transportation services, and recreational programs are some of the basic services offered by community organizations. Some organizations also offer home health care. With nurses and aides assigned to visit the elderly in their homes and to help them with their housework and medical needs, elderly clients can continue to live on their own.

Geriatric social workers evaluate clients by interviewing them and determining their needs; social workers then enroll clients for these services. They make phone calls and provide the service agencies with client information.

The client may need even more assistance. Adult day care services are available in some cities, as are adult foster care services that match older people with families. A social worker may also need to help a client arrange to move into a nursing home and counsel the client about the transition. These counseling services are also extended to members of the client's family, advising them in how to deal with a parent's or grandparent's aging or illness.

In some cases, an elderly person is neglected or taken advantage of. A geriatric social worker can look into these cases and serve as an advocate, stepping in to advise the client of his or her legal rights. In addition to legal services, a geriatric social worker will help a client locate any needed financial services. Social workers help clients make arrangements for the payment of services through Medicare and other financial aid.

Because of efforts by the government to improve the quality of nursing home care, social workers are becoming more active within these facilities. These geriatric social workers work closely with the elderly and their families in arranging the move into the nursing home. They also counsel families upon the death of an elderly relative and help with funeral arrangements. Geriatric social workers also protect and promote the rights of the residents, and they may conduct in-services with nursing care staff members on patient rights.

The geriatric social worker is part of the larger field of aging. This field—which works to provide help for older people while researching the process of aging—is composed of hospitals, health care corporations, government agencies, churches, colleges, and other organizations and institutions. Various professions, such as law, psychology, health care, education, and marketing, include specialties in aging, or gerontology.

Requirements

High School

Since you will need at least a bachelor's degree to advance in this field, prepare for college by taking a college prep curriculum. This should include math, science, and computer science classes. Other courses that will help you in this field include civics or government courses, in which you can learn about the enactment of laws, such as the Older Americans Act. Psychology and sociology courses will help you gain an understanding of human behavior and the process of aging as well as teach you methods for studying groups of people, such as the elderly. Take English classes to develop your writing, speaking, and researching skills—skills that you will need throughout your career.

Postsecondary Training

Although you may be able to work in some levels of geriatric social work with only a high school diploma or associate's degree, most professional opportunities exist for people with bachelor's or more advanced degrees in social work. The Council on Social Work Education, which accredits bachelor's and master's programs in social work, has given accredition to over 450 programs granting the bachelor's degree in social work (B.S.W.) and over 150 programs granting the master's degree (M.S.W.). The council offers the *Directory of Colleges and Universities with Accredited Social Work Degree Programs,* providing contact information. In addition, the council's Web site (http://www.cswe.org) has a member program directory that lists accredited programs by state. The Group for the Advancement of Doctoral Education provides contact information for over 60 programs that offer the doctor of social work degree (D.S.W.) or Ph.D.s in social work (visit the Web site at http://www.sc.edu/swan/gade). Accredited B.S.W. programs will include courses in human behavior and the social environment; social welfare policy and services; social work practice; research; and field practicum. Most programs require two years of liberal arts study, followed by two years of study in the social work major. Students must also complete a field practicum of at least 400 hours.

Although no clear lines of classification are drawn in the social work profession, most supervisory and administrative positions require at least a master's degree in social work. Master's programs are organized according to fields of practice (such as mental health care), problem areas (substance abuse), population groups (the elderly), and practice roles (practice with individuals, families, or communities). They are usually two-year programs, requiring at least 900 hours of field practice.

Some programs allow students at the master's level to specialize in gerontology. The Council on Social Work Education offers the annual publication, *Summary Information on Master of Social Work Programs*, providing information on master's programs. Doctoral degrees prepare students for research and teaching. Most social workers with doctorates go to work in community organizations.

Certification or Licensing

The National Association of Social Workers (NASW) offers certification in several areas. All social workers who meet requirements including education, experience, and passing an exam may receive the designation Academy of Certified Social Workers. In addition, NASW offers specialty certifications and certification as a Qualified Clincial Social Worker and as a Diplomate in Clinical Social Work to those who meet specific education, practice, and other requirements. Although certification is voluntary, it is highly recommended for anyone wanting to advance in the field. Certification demonstrates that you have gained the knowledge and experience necessary to meet national standards.

The practice of social work is regulated in all states. To receive the necessary licensing, a social worker will typically have to gain a certain amount of experience and also pass an exam. Because requirements vary by state, you will need to check with the regulatory board in your state for specific information. Licensing information is also available from the Association of Social Work Boards.

Other Requirements

To be a successful geriatric social worker, you must care about the needs and problems of older people. Many of these people will be relying on you to help them through crucial and difficult times; you must be completely dedicated to your clients and devoted to helping them maintain their dignity and sense of self-worth.

Most geriatric social workers are involved directly with the people they serve, and they are expected to carefully examine a client's living habits and family relations. A geriatric social worker has to be prepared to confront depressing situations occasionally. In most cases, though, a good geriatric social worker will take pleasure from helping a client through a rough time and will take pride in seeing the client improve his or her life. It is also important for a geriatric social worker to be good-natured and friendly; clients resistant to change may refuse to cooperate with someone they find unpleasant. A geriatric social worker must be very sensitive to the problems of the elderly but must also remain supportive and encouraging.

Exploring

Volunteering is one of the best ways to explore your interest in geriatric social work. Check with nursing homes, senior care centers, or other organizations, such as Meals on Wheels, in your area for volunteer opportunities. Another way to gain experience is to get summer or part-time work at a local hospital, nursing home, or home health care agency. Home health care aides have the opportunity to work closely with the elderly and to get to know their needs and concerns. Also, as a college student enrolled in a social work program, you may have the opportunity to help a faculty member with a gerontological research project.

Employers

Opportunities for geriatric social workers can be found in both the public and private sectors. Hospitals, nursing homes, retirement communities, human services offices, senior centers, and government agencies all employ geriatric social workers. With so many services available for older people, there are a variety of job opportunities for the geriatric social worker. There are some agencies that may deal only with the practical aspects of aiding older people—arranging for services and managing financial and legal issues. Working for other agencies may involve the organization of recreational and educational activities, such as senior theater groups and art classes.

Starting Out

After receiving your social work degree and gaining some field experience, you will have made valuable connections among faculty and social service organizations. These connections may be able to help you find a job. Your college's job placement service or internship program may also direct you to your first full-time position. You should also become familiar with the local senior centers and agencies for the elderly.

Joining a professional organization can be helpful in entering the field. The American Society on Aging sponsors a job bank and publishes newsletters. Job opportunities are listed in the newsletters of the American Geriatrics Society, the American Counseling Association, and other professional organizations. You should also attend annual meetings, which give you the chance to meet other people working in social work, geriatrics, and gerontology.

Advancement

Most geriatric social workers enter the field focusing on the work rather than on the promotions and salary raises. However, there are advancement opportunities for dedicated social workers. Successful social workers may move up the ranks of their organizations to become supervisors or directors, taking on additional responsibilities such as overseeing new hires. A key factor in achieving the most advanced positions is to have advanced education. Those who move into the higher-paid positions in administration, program development, or policy analysis must have a Ph.D. or, in some cases, a master's degree with practical experience.

Within smaller agencies and in smaller towns, advancement opportunities may be few, but there may also be less competition for these jobs. A greater number of advancement opportunities may be available in service organizations in urban areas.

Earnings

The more advanced a person's degree is, the more he or she can make in the social work profession. Typically, work with the elderly has paid less than other areas of social work, such as mental health and community planning. The region of the United States in which a geriatric social worker is employed also influences salaries. For example, geriatric social workers can make more money on the East and West Coasts than in the Midwest.

An Economic Research Institute study in 1999 found that geriatric social workers just starting out in the field earned between approximately $24,000 and $32,520 per year. Geriatric social workers with nine years of work experience made between approximately $34,250 and $46,395; and those with 18 years of experience made between approximately $43,470 and $58,880 annually. Geriatric social workers holding a master's degree and employed by the federal government started out with the rating of GS-10. This rating had a salary range of approximately $36,620 to $47,610 in 2001.

Benefits will depend on the employer, but they generally include health insurance and paid vacation time.

Work Environment

Although geriatric social workers do spend some time in an office setting, they spend much of their time interviewing clients and the directors of programs; they also visit the homes of their clients to evaluate and take notes. They may also visit the homes of clients' families. Although some geriatric social workers may work in hospital and nursing home environments, others have their offices in human service agencies alongside other service providers. Serving as an advocate for the elderly client requires, in addition to phone calls and faxes, personal meetings with directors of agencies, local legislators, and others. In cases of abuse and neglect, it may require testifying in court.

Because poverty and illness afflict a large number of people over the age of 65, the geriatric social worker is often assigned depressing, seemingly hopeless cases. This may be the situation only temporarily, however, as the social worker introduces the client to the necessary services and assistance.

Outlook

The field of social work is expected to grow faster than the average through 2008, according to the U.S. Department of Labor. Those specializing in geriatric social work—a career *U.S. News & World Report* listed on its hot job track for 2000—will be in great demand for several reasons. It is estimated that, as people live longer (more than 15 million people in the United States will be over the age of 85 by the middle of the 21st century), more geriatric social workers will be needed to create programs and provide services for the growing number of elderly persons. Rising health care costs are causing many insurance companies to consider alternatives to hospital treatment, so some insurance coverage now includes home stays. In addition, hospitals and nursing homes are trying to balance the demand for their services and their limitations in staff and physical facilities. As home care becomes a viable, affordable option for more older people, more geriatric social workers will be necessary to evaluate the needs of clients and set up services.

The Omnibus Budget Reconciliation Act passed by the U. S. Congress in 1987 to improve nursing home care requires large nursing care facilities to employ full-time social workers. As the government becomes more involved in providing better care for the elderly, the geriatric social worker will see more full-time job opportunities in nursing homes and hospitals.

For More Information

To read Careers in Aging, *visit the following Web site:*

Association for Gerontology in Higher Education
1030 15th Street, NW, Suite 240
Washington, DC 20005-1503
Tel: 202-289-9806
Web: http://www.aghe.org

For information on licensing, contact:

Association of Social Work Boards
400 South Ridge Parkway, Suite B
Culpeper, VA 22701
Tel: 800-225-6880
Email: info@aswb.org
Web: http://www.aswb.org

For information on education and the field of social work, contact:

Council on Social Work Education
1725 Duke Street, Suite 500
Alexandria, VA 22314-3457
Tel: 703-683-8080
Email: info@cswe.org
Web: http://www.cswe.org

For certification information and to read Choices: Careers in Social Work, *visit the following Web site:*

National Association of Social Workers
750 First Street, NE, Suite 700
Washington, DC 20002-4241
Tel: 800-638-8799
Web: http://www.naswdc.org

For more information on careers in geriatric social work, contact the following organizations:

American Association of Homes and Services for the Aging
2519 Connecticut Avenue, NW
Washington, DC 20008-1520
Tel: 202-783-2242
Web: http://www.aahsa.org

American Geriatrics Society
350 Fifth Avenue, Suite 801
New York, NY 10118
Tel: 212-308-1414
Email: info@americangeriatrics.org
Web: http://www.americangeriatrics.org

American Society on Aging
833 Market Street, Suite 511
San Francisco, CA 94103-1824
Tel: 415-974-9600
Email: info@asaging.org
Web: http://www.asaging.org

Gerontological Society of America
1030 15th Street, NW, Suite 250
Washington, DC 20005
Tel: 202-842-1275
Web: http://www.geron.org

Grief Therapists

School Subjects	Psychology Sociology
Personal Skills	Communication/ideas Helping/teaching
Work Environment	Primarily indoors Primarily one location
Minimum Education Level	Master's degree
Salary Range	$35,000 to $45,000 to $60,000+
Certification or Licensing	Required by certain states
Outlook	Faster than the average

Overview

A *grief therapist* or *bereavement counselor* offers therapy for those who are mourning the death of a family member or a loved one. Therapists help survivors work through possible feelings of anger or guilt and help them recover from their loss. Counselors may be brought into communities or facilities to help individuals after a national disaster, act of violence, or an accident. Grief therapists may be self-employed as independent counselors or work for hospitals, funeral homes, schools, hospice organizations, nursing homes, or government and private agencies.

History

Grief therapy is a relatively new career specialty. According to Dr. Dana Cable, professor of psychology at Hood College in Frederick, Maryland, and a certified grief therapist, "Grief therapy is a growing area because of the nature of many deaths today. There are many more issues to be worked through when we lose young people to violent deaths and diseases such as

AIDS. In addition, there is some movement away from organized religion where people used to find comfort when they lost a loved one." Cable also points out that changes in the family unit have affected the way in which family members grieve. Many families are not close, physically or emotionally, resulting in issues of guilt when a family member dies. Another factor that has boosted growth is that people today are more willing to accept the help of a therapist than in years past.

In a 1998 career guide, *U.S. News & World Report* listed grief therapy as one of 20 hot jobs. The field has grown as baby boomers are facing the death of friends and parents.

The Job

Grief therapists help individuals accept the death of a spouse, child, partner, parent, sibling, or loved one. The therapist gives his or her clients reassurance and helps them resolve negative feelings that may be associated with the death. Counseling may be done on a one-to-one basis, with a small group, or as part of a support group.

When disasters such as accidents or violence occur, grief therapists are often brought in to speak to communities, schools, or organizations. They help people deal with the tragedy and may provide individual counseling. In recent times, therapists have been called upon when violence has hit schools, when weather-related tragedies have destroyed communities, or after airplane crashes or terrorist bombings.

Hospitals, nursing homes, AIDS and cancer care centers, and hospice organizations employ grief therapists to provide emotional support to patients and their families and friends. In addition, some funeral homes refer families and friends to grief therapists as part of an after-care service following a funeral.

Grief therapists also work as *death educators*. These specialists conduct classes for people who work in professions that deal with the sick and dying, such as medical and nursing students. They may also speak to organizations, clubs, support groups, parents, and others about issues related to death and give them suggestions on how they can cope or how they can help someone who is grieving deal with their loss.

Requirements

High School

College prep classes are essential if you wish to enter the field of grief therapy. In order to learn how to deal with a diverse group of people from all cultural backgrounds, courses in health, sociology, psychology, and religion would be helpful. Communication is a key part of the grief therapist's job, so speech, foreign languages, communication, and English courses are also vital. It may be a good idea to check with the colleges you have selected to find out what courses they recommend for a career in psychology and counseling.

Postsecondary Training

Degrees that are strong in psychology, or a pre-med program are usually recommended for counselors. This must be followed with a master's program in counseling, social work, or psychology. Following this with a doctoral degree in psychology is recommended for the best job prospects.

Certification and Licensing

The Association for Death Education and Counseling is currently revising their certification program to include two levels of credentialing. A certificate program will be available to those just entering the field, while a higher level of certification will be offered to those with advanced degrees and experience.

Some states require grief therapists to obtain licenses in order to practice. These licensing requirements may vary from state to state, so it is best to check with the state in which you plan to practice. Some states may limit counselors' private practices to areas in which they have developed professional competence. There may also be some continuing education requirements for license renewal.

Other Requirements

If you are interested in becoming a grief therapist, you should enjoy work-ing with people and feel comfortable dealing with the sick and dying. You should show patience and be a compassionate listener, as well as be able to express yourself clearly and tactfully.

A grief therapist must not let their job take an emotional toll on their own life. Though they hear many stories of grief and sadness, therapists can also find their job rewarding and uplifting as they help people overcome feel-ings of depression and despair and continue on with their lives.

Exploring

Your high school guidance counselor may be able to supply information on a career as a therapist. Other sources for information can be found at your local or school library, or through the Internet. Contact the organizations list-ed at the end of this article for further information.

Doing volunteer work for organizations such as the Red Cross, or with your local hospital, nursing home, or hospice care center will give you more experience dealing with the sick, troubled, or grieving. Participating in high school clubs or other groups that organize volunteer projects to benefit homeless people, victims of AIDS, or battered spouses can also give you valu-able experience.

Employers

Grief therapists may provide grief therapy as an independent part of their larger counseling practice, or they may work as part of an organization. Many grief therapists in private practice offer grief therapy. Some therapists are part of a group practice of medical or psychological professionals who offer a vari-ety of counseling and therapy services. Funeral homes, nursing homes, assisted care facilities, AIDS care facilities, hospice organizations, and almost any facility or organization that deals with the sick and dying use grief ther-apists. Many have a therapist either on call or on staff. The government may also employ counselors and grief therapists in their health care facilities.

Some grief therapists may work under contract with large corporations as part of employee assistance programs. Others may be called upon by airlines, schools, communities, or businesses at times of crises or when violence has occurred. They may also work on a contract basis to make presentations or seminars to various groups or organizations.

Grief therapists may also work at colleges or universities, conducting research or teaching classes that deal with death and grief.

Starting Out

Some colleges and universities offer job placement for people seeking careers in counseling. While in graduate school, therapy students often work as interns with hospitals, hospices, health care, or crisis-care organizations, or with therapists in private practices. These relationships can often offer employment and networking possibilities after graduation.

Most grief therapists practice general counseling before specializing in grief therapy. Building a client base as a counselor can help provide the base for beginning a career in grief therapy. Personal contacts can also provide networking possibilities. Membership in a professional counseling association may offer sources for contacts and help you find job leads. Classified advertisements and trade magazines also list job openings.

Advancement

Counselors specializing in grief therapy can advance to head their own counseling service or group practice, serving clients directly or contracting out services to hospitals, businesses, hospice organizations, and other facilities. Experienced grief therapists who specialize in education can become department heads of universities or colleges. Counselors with a business background and experience can advance to become executive directors of health care facilities, organizations, nursing homes, or head professional organizations that serve the counseling profession.

Earnings

The salary range for grief therapists is generally the same as for other therapists and counselors. Beginning therapists can expect to make around $35,000. More experienced counselors can make about $45,000, with some earnings reaching $60,000. Some counselors in private practice and those who become directors of facilities may earn considerably more.

Benefits may vary depending on the position and the employer but generally vacation, sick leave, insurance and other work related benefits are typical. Persons who are self-employed usually have to provide their own insurance and retirement funds.

Work Environment

Generally, grief therapists work in office settings that are clean and well lighted. Grief therapists who work in crisis situations will find a wide variety of working environments depending on the situation, but usually small, temporary offices are set up to accommodate counselors.

Counselors in private or group practice may have to set up evening and weekend office hours. Some grief counseling must be done on an emergency basis in times of crisis or violence, so there may be occasions when counselors have to drop everything to work any time of the day or night.

Many counselors stick to a given location to serve the local community. However, depending on the type and range of cases the therapist handles, travel may be necessary, including nights and weekends.

Outlook

According to the U.S. Department of Labor, employment opportunities in the counseling field are expected to grow faster than the average for all occupations through 2008. Demand should be strongest for counselors concentrating on rehabilitation and mental health—the latter including grief therapy.

A career in grief therapy holds great promise. Our changing and aging society creates a need for grief counseling. As baby boomers age and experience the death of their parents and friends and family, they are seeking the help of bereavement counselors to help them adjust and deal with their feelings. Counseling has become a socially accepted tool to help people deal with difficult or painful situations.

As violent crimes occur and as young people witness acts of violence and experience the untimely death of friends, they seek an understanding that grief counselors can help provide. Car accidents, AIDS, and drug-related deaths can also create feelings of guilt and depression that counselors can help people work through. Unfortunately, there will continue to be natural disasters such as tornadoes, floods, avalanches, and earthquakes that kill large numbers of people. Grief counselors will continue to be called on to help ease survivors' pain.

Although grief therapists work in every part of the country, demand is highest in retirement areas of the country where there is a large elderly population.

For More Information

For career and certification information, contact the following organizations:

American Counseling Association
5999 Stevenson Avenue
Alexandria, VA 22304-3300
Tel: 703-823-9800
Web: http://www.counseling.org/

Association for Death Education and Counseling
342 North Main Street
West Hartford, CT 06117-2507
Tel: 860-586-7503
Web: http://www.adec.org

For information on working with grieving children and their families, contact:

Dougy Center
National Center for Grieving Children and Families
PO Box 86852
Portland, OR 97286
Tel: 503-775-5683
Web: http://www.dougy.org

For information on graduate programs in thanatology, or the study of grief ther-apy, contact these colleges:

College of New Rochelle
Graduate School, Division of Human Services
29 Castle Place
New Rochelle, NY 10805
Tel: 914-654-5561
Email: gs@cnr.edu
Web: http://cnr.edu/

Hood College
401 Rosemont Avenue
Frederick, MD 21701-8575
Tel: 301-663-3131
Email: hoodgrad@hood.edu
Web: http://www.hood.edu

HIV/AIDS Counselors and Case Managers

School Subjects
Health
Psychology
Sociology

Personal Skills
Communication/ideas
Helping/teaching

Work Environment
Primarily indoors
Primarily one location

Minimum Education Level
Bachelor's degree

Salary Range
$19,250 to $30,590 to $49,080

Certification or Licensing
Required by certain states

Outlook
Faster than the average

Overview

HIV/AIDS counselors and case managers work with people who are infected with HIV (Human Immunodeficiency Virus) or have developed AIDS (Acquired Immune Deficiency Syndrome), and with their families and friends, to help them cope with the physical and emotional results of the disease. They answer questions, offer advice and support, and help HIV/AIDS patients get necessary assistance from medical and social agencies.

History

No one knows the exact origin of HIV, though there are several different theories. The virus has existed in the United States, Haiti, and Africa since at least 1977 or 1978. In 1979, doctors in Los Angeles and New York began to diagnose and report rare types of pneumonia, cancer, and other illnesses not usually found in persons with healthy immune systems.

The Centers for Disease Control and Prevention (CDC) officially named the condition AIDS (Acquired Immune Deficiency Syndrome) in 1982. In 1984, the virus responsible for weakening the immune system was identified as HIV (Human Immunodeficiency Virus).

Today, the CDC estimates that approximately 800,000 to 900,000 Americans are living with HIV, and at least 40,000 new infections occur each year. The professions of HIV/AIDS counselor and case manager developed in the mid-1980s as a division of social work.

The Job

HIV/AIDS counselors and case managers help HIV and AIDS patients deal with their illness in the best way possible. A person who has tested positive for HIV or who has been diagnosed as having AIDS has many issues to deal with. Some of the issues are similar to those faced by anyone diagnosed with a terminal illness—grief, fear, and concerns over health care, financial planning, and making provisions for children or other family members. Other issues these patients may face are unique to HIV and AIDS sufferers. These may include discrimination, prejudice, and exclusion by family and acquaintances who are afraid of or do not understand the disease. Another special consideration for these patients is how to avoid passing the disease on to others.

Counselors and case managers offer support and assistance in dealing with all the various social, physical, and emotional issues patients face. Together counselors and case managers work with clients in all stages of the disease—from those who have first tested positive for HIV to those who are in the final stages of the illness. They may work at HIV testing centers, public health clinics, mental health clinics, family planning clinics, hospitals, and drug treatment facilities.

Counselors who work at testing facilities, sometimes called *test counselors*, work with individuals who are being tested for HIV. These counselors usually meet with clients before they are tested to find out about the client's level of risk for the disease, to explain the testing procedure, and to talk about what the possible test results mean. They also explain how the HIV infection is spread, discuss ways to prevent it, and answer general questions about the disease and its progress.

Results from the test are typically available a few days to two weeks after the client has had the initial meeting. When the client returns to find out the results, the counselor again meets with him or her. If the results are negative, the counselor may suggest re-testing if, during the six months before the test, the client engaged in any behaviors that might have resulted in infection. Since the infection does not show up immediately after it is contracted, it is possible to be infected and still test negative.

If the results are positive, the counselor talks with the client about his or her sexual activity and drug use to determine how they might have gotten the disease. They also help them decide whom to notify of the test results, such as previous sex partners.

At some testing clinics, such as those offering STD (sexually transmitted disease) testing as well as HIV testing, a client initially meets with a nurse who conducts the test. In these circumstances, when the client returns for the test results he or she may then meet with an HIV counselor if necessary.

The counselor is often the first person the HIV-positive client talks to about the illness. A large part of the job, then, is referring the client to appropriate sources of help, including AIDS-related agencies, social services, and health care providers.

Case managers, unlike counselors, follow patients through the various stages of their illness, helping them coordinate and manage the resources necessary to deal with it. In some instances, case managers may not begin working with a client until that client has developed AIDS. Through letters, phone calls, and contacts with a network of available service providers, case managers help their clients get access to the agencies or organizations that offer the assistance they need. Assistance may include medical care, legal help, help with living expenses, or visits by home health care aides.

People with HIV and AIDS are under severe emotional strain. In addition to coping with the physical effects of the disease, they must also cope with the burden of having a disease that much of society does not understand or accept. They may feel anger, depression, guilt, and shame as they learn to live with their disease.

Counselors and case managers help clients deal with these emotional strains. They may conduct AIDS support groups or group counseling sessions in which HIV or AIDS patients discuss their experiences and questions about living with the disease. In these group sessions, the counselor or case manager oversees the conversation and tries to move it in a positive direction.

HIV/AIDS counselors and case managers may also work with the family members, friends, and partners of those with HIV or AIDS, either in individual or group sessions. They may meet with family members or partners to discuss the client's progress or to help them understand their loved one's needs. They may also set up and oversee grief counseling sessions for those who have lost relatives or partners to the disease.

In order to monitor clients' progress, case managers keep written records on each of their sessions. They may be required to participate in staff meetings to discuss a client's progress and treatment plan. They may also meet with members of various social service agencies to discuss their clients' needs.

In addition to the primary duty of counseling clients, these workers may participate in community efforts to increase HIV and AIDS awareness. They may help develop workshops, give speeches to high schools or other groups, or organize and lead public awareness campaigns.

Requirements

High School

If you are considering a career in the field of HIV/AIDS counseling, you should emphasize sociology and psychology classes in your curriculum. Because this area of counseling requires an understanding of how the human body is affected by the HIV and AIDS viruses, you should also take classes such as biology, physiology, and health. To develop your communication skills, take English classes. You may also want to take a foreign language, which will give you the ability to communicate with non-English speakers.

Postsecondary Training

Although specific educational requirements for HIV/AIDS counselors and case managers vary, most employers require a bachelor's degree in mental health, counseling, or social work. Some employers may require their employees to have a master's degree. A college-level curriculum for a degree in mental health or social work is likely to include classes in counseling, sociology, psychology, human development, and mental health. Your college education will also include a minimum of 400 hours of supervised field work, known as a practicum. The Council on Social Work Education (CSWE) is the only accrediting body for bachelor's and master's degree programs in social work in the United States. When selecting a program to attend, make sure it is CSWE approved. To view a listing of such programs, go to the Member Program Directory on the CSWE Web site: http://www.cswe.org. You can also order the printed version, *Directory of*

Colleges and Universities with Accredited Social Work Degree Programs. The master's degree in social work allows you to concentrate your studies on your field of practice. These programs usually last two or two and a half years and require supervised field work of at least 900 hours.

Some employers will hire job candidates with bachelor's degrees in other fields, such as education. To prepare yourself for this work, however, you should include such classes as psychology and health in your coursework. Gaining work experience will be essential for you, so look for internships or summer jobs that offer the opportunity to combine your interests, for example in public health education or with an HIV/AIDS service organization. If you cannot find a paid position, you can still strengthen your resume by doing volunteer work at an HIV/AIDS organization; many are involved in such areas as advocacy, education, and home support services.

Certification or Licensing

Most states require some form of credentialing for HIV/AIDS counselors and case managers. Many choose to be certified by the National Board for Certified Counselors. To become certified, candidates must have completed a master's degree in counseling, have at least two years of professional experience, and pass a national examination. Upon successful completion of these requirements, the candidate is designated as a National Certified Counselor. Additionally, all states require some form of licensing, registration, or certification for anyone working as a social worker. Requirements vary by state, so you will need to check with your state's licensing board for specific information.

Other Requirements

Because these diseases receive so much attention from the medical, social, and even government arenas, there are often new developments in HIV- and AIDS-related treatments, policies, and services. In order to keep up-to-date, counselors and case managers must regularly continue their education by attending seminars or monthly in-service meetings.

For individuals considering a career in HIV/AIDS counseling, certain personal qualifications may be just as important as having the correct educational background. Compassion, sensitivity, and the desire to help others are key qualities for these counselors. They must also be able to communicate effectively and sincerely and to listen with understanding.

HIV/AIDS counselors and case managers must be emotionally stable and resilient in order to keep from becoming depressed and discouraged by the nature of their work. They need to be able to avoid becoming too emotionally involved with their patients by balancing empathy with objectivity.

Exploring

If you are interested in a career in HIV/AIDS counseling, you might contact local hospitals, HIV testing centers, or AIDS service organizations for more information. It may be possible to meet with a counselor to talk about the details of his or her job. Any school or local library should also have a large number of resources both on the AIDS virus and on counseling. You can also use the Internet to get the latest information about HIV and AIDS by visiting such sources as the Centers for Disease Control and Prevention (http://www.cdc.gov) and the HIV/AIDS Bureau of the Health Services Resources Administration (http://www.hab.hrsa.gov).

To further explore the career, you may be able to find a volunteer position in a social service agency, health clinic, or hospital. Even if the position does not deal directly with HIV or AIDS patients, it should provide you with an idea of what it is like to work in such an environment. Once you have graduated from high school, you may be eligible to join the National AIDS Fund AmeriCorps Program, which trains participants to do HIV/AIDS education and counseling and places them in selected cities for approximately 11 months of service. (See the end of this article for the Fund's contact information.)

Employers

HIV/AIDS counselors and case managers work for hospitals, hospices, HIV testing centers, public health clinics, mental health clinics, social service agencies, Red Cross offices, Planned Parenthood centers, and various AIDS service organizations. They may also work for regional AIDS consortia organized by health officials, religious leaders, educators, business leaders, and AIDS service representatives.

Starting Out

New graduates may begin their job searches at the career placement centers of their colleges. They might also apply directly to any area social service, health, or AIDS service organizations. Some openings for HIV/AIDS counselors or case managers might be advertised in the classified sections of local newspapers. Membership in a professional organization, such as the American Counseling Association, might also provide the job seeker with leads through publications, meetings, or job banks. Additionally, graduates may look for internship opportunities, such as the University of California-San Francisco AIDS Health Project's Internship Program. This year-long program offers new college graduates focused education and experience in HIV care. Through such internships, graduates can hone professional skills as well as make professional contacts that may lead to later full-time employment.

Advancement

Counselors and case managers who work for large organizations will have more opportunity for advancement than those who work for smaller ones. In a large organization, for example, the counselor with education and experience might move into an administrative position, such as program director. Because smaller organizations—especially not-for-profit organizations—usually have small staffs, advancement is often slow and limited.

Those who continue their education may have a wider range of possibilities for advancement. Counselors who complete master's degrees in social work or rehabilitative counseling, for example, might be employed by social welfare agencies as medical or psychiatric social workers, child protective workers, rehabilitative counselors, or parole or probation officers. These fields have a broader scope of advancement opportunities.

Finally, some who continue their education elect to go into research or teaching at the college level.

Earnings

Generally, earnings for HIV/AIDS counselors and case managers are similar to those for other counselors and social workers. Salaries can vary, however, depending upon the experience and education of the individual and the location, size, and funding source of the employer. The U.S. Department of

Labor reported the median yearly earnings of all social workers as $30,590 in 1998. The lowest paid 10 percent made less than $19,250 per year, while the highest paid 10 percent earned more than $49,080. Those at the top end of the pay scale typically have extensive experience and advanced degrees and work at well-funded programs. For example, in June 2001, the University of California-San Francisco AIDS Health Project posted a job opening for a clinical social worker II, which required the applicant to have a master's degree in psychology, counseling, or social work. The job responsibilities included providing HIV training for test counselors, developing resource materials, and scheduling training sessions. The starting salary for this position was approximately $47,520.

In addition to salary, most HIV/AIDS counselors and case managers receive a benefits package that includes paid vacations, holidays, and sick time, medical insurance, and sometimes a retirement plan.

Work Environment

HIV/AIDS counselors and case managers usually work regular eight-hour days, five days a week. Occasionally, however, they may have appointments with health care providers, social service agencies, or patients outside of regular office hours.

Counselors who work in HIV testing centers and health clinics usually have on-site offices where they can talk privately with clients. Those who work as case managers may visit clients in their homes or in hospitals or other long-range care facilities. They may conduct group sessions in classrooms or conference rooms of hospitals or social service agencies. Regardless of the setting, HIV/AIDS counselors and case managers spend a majority of their day meeting with people—either clients and family members or representatives from social service or health care agencies.

Counseling those with HIV and AIDS is stressful and often depressing work. In most cases, clients are preparing for eventual death, and they turn to the counseling professional for help and support in facing it. Case managers often watch their clients become very sick as the virus progresses; frequently, they must deal with clients' deaths. Dealing with this sickness, death, and the accompanying emotional distress on a daily basis may be difficult.

Outlook

Employment trends for HIV/AIDS counselors and case managers are likely to depend upon government funding for AIDS-related programs, since private funding for such programs is usually limited. Government funding for health programs, however, fluctuates, and resistance from some special interest groups or policy makers may negatively influence spending on AIDS research and programs. Nevertheless, the U.S. Department of Labor predicts the employment outlook for social workers, who are closely related professionals, to be much faster than the average through 2008. Additional factors influencing job opportunities for HIV/AIDS counselors and case managers include the continued spread of HIV, the increased number of people living longer with HIV than in previous years, and the new complications (medical, financial, and even social) that are brought on by new treatments. Given all of these various factors, experts predict the employment outlook for HIV/AIDS counselors to be on the increase.

These professionals can play an especially important role in educating the public at large and those with HIV and AIDS on how to cope with the disease and avoid its spread. Jobs for HIV/AIDS counselors and case managers will probably be most plentiful in urban areas, with their larger populations. Those with the most current knowledge and HIV/AIDS training will find the best opportunities.

For More Information

For information about counseling and graduate programs in counseling, contact:

American Counseling Association
5999 Stevenson Avenue
Alexandria, VA 22304-3300
Tel: 800-347-6647
Web: http://www.counseling.org

For information about HIV and AIDS, contact the following organizations:

Centers for Disease Control and Prevention
1600 Clifton Road
Atlanta, GA 30333
Tel: 800-311-3435 or 800-342-2437 (National AIDS Hotline)
Web: http://www.cdc.gov

Health Services Resources Administration
HIV/AIDS Bureau
5600 Fishers Lane, Room 11A-33
Rockville, MD 20857
Tel: 301-443-6652
Web: http://www.hab.hrsa.gov

For information on education and certification, contact the following organizations:

National Association of Social Workers
750 First Street, NE, Suite 700
Washington, DC 20002-4241
Tel: 800-638-8799
Email: info@naswdc.org
Web: http://www.naswdc.org

National Board for Certified Counselors
3 Terrace Way, Suite D
Greensboro, NC 27403-3660
Tel: 336-547-0607
Email: nbcc@nbcc.org
Web: http://www.nbcc.org/

For more information on this AmeriCorps program, contact:

National AIDS Fund AmeriCorps Program
1030 15th Street, NW
Washington, DC 20005
Tel: 888-234-AIDS
Web: http://www.aidsfund.org/americorp.htm

Home Health Care Aides

School Subjects	Family and consumer science Health
Personal Skills	Helping/teaching
Work Environment	Primarily indoors Primarily multiple locations
Minimum Education Level	High school diploma
Salary Range	$10,000 to $16,640 to $34,000
Certification or Licensing	Voluntary
Outlook	Much faster than the average

Overview

Home health care aides, also known as *homemaker-home health aides* or *home attendants,* serve elderly and infirm persons by visiting them in their homes and caring for them. Working under the supervision of nurses or social workers, they perform various household chores that clients are unable to perform for themselves as well as attend to patients' personal needs. Although they work primarily with the elderly, home health care aides also attend to clients with disabilities or those needing help with small children.

History

Family photographs from the last century frequently included a grandparent posed alongside the children or an elderly aunt or uncle arm-in-arm with a niece or nephew. A typical household of the time often counted an elderly parent or ill or injured relative among its members. Without most of the modern conveniences we take for granted today, day-to-day living and regular household chores could be impossible for someone weakened by illness or age. It was often expected for parents to move in with children when they became unable to look after themselves; sometimes a room was prepared and waiting for them long in advance. In rural situations, elderly parents might have been expected to give up the homestead to a child or grandchild once they became incapable of looking after the place themselves.

Those without families were sometimes confined to hospitals or sanatoriums. People with contagious diseases or disabilities who required constant supervision were also cared for in institutions. Even with family, however, the needs of the elderly or infirm person often exceeded the facilities, time, and energy that the family had to offer. The business of running a household left little time for the family to tend to the needs of the terminally or seriously ill.

Rural areas often made "visiting nurses" available to check on patients who lived far from town and lacked regular transportation for medical visits. These nurses eventually discovered that the needs of the patients went beyond medical care. Patients were grateful for the company of another person in their homes, someone to read their mail to them or run errands. They were grateful not to have to abandon their own homes just because they needed a little assistance from time to time. As the demand for this kind of home care advanced, home attendants found that people needed their services, and the profession of home care aides began to grown.

Advances in modern medicine have made it possible for many illnesses to be treated at home. Hospitals and stores now rent items such as wheelchairs and oxygen tanks, enabling people to have medical equipment available in their own homes. The medical profession is also learning how a person's recovery and treatment can be affected by his or her environment. People generally recover from illnesses better when they are treated in their home environment. The number of home care agencies has grown from about 1,100 in 1963 to over 20,000 today.

The Job

Home health care aides enable elderly persons to stay in their own homes. For some clients, just a few visits a week are enough to help them look after themselves. Although physically demanding, the work is often emotionally rewarding. Home care aides may not have access to equipment and facilities such as those found in hospitals, but they also don't have the hospital's frantic pace. Home care aides are expected to take the time to get to know their clients and their individual needs. They perform their duties within the client's home environment, which often is a much better atmosphere than the impersonal rooms of a hospital.

In addition to the elderly, home health care aides assist people of any age who are recovering at home following hospitalization. They also help children whose parents are ill, disabled, or neglectful. Aides may be trained to supply care to people suffering from specific illnesses such as AIDS, Alzheimer's disease, or cancer, or patients who are developmentally disabled and lack sufficient daily living skills.

Clients unable to feed themselves may depend on home care aides to shop for food, prepare meals, feed them, and clean up after meals. Likewise, home health care aides may assist clients in dressing and grooming, including bathing, cleaning teeth and nails, and fixing the clients' hair.

Massages, alcohol rubs, whirlpool baths, and other therapies and treatments may be a part of a client's required care. Home health care aides may work closely with a physician or home nurse in giving medications and dietary supplements and helping with exercises and other therapies. They may check pulses, temperatures, and respiration rates. Occasionally, they may change nonsterile dressings, use special equipment such as a hydraulic lift, or assist with braces or artificial limbs.

Home health care aides working in home care agencies are supervised by a registered nurse, physical therapist, or social worker who assigns them specific duties. Aides report changes in patients' conditions to these supervisors.

Household chores are often another aspect of the home health care aide's responsibilities. Light housekeeping, such as changing bed linens, doing the laundry and ironing, and dusting, may be necessary. When a home care aide looks after the children of a disabled or neglectful parent, work may include making lunches for the children, helping them with their homework, or providing companionship and adult supervision in the evening.

Personal attention and comfort are important aspects of an aide's care. Home health care aides can provide this support by reading to children, playing checkers, or visiting with an elderly client. Often just listening to a client's personal problems will help the client through the day. Because elderly people do not always have the means to venture out alone, a home health care aide may accompany an ambulatory patient to the park for an afternoon stroll or to the physician's office for an appointment.

Requirements

High School

Many programs require only a high school diploma for entry-level positions. Previous or additional coursework in home economics, cooking, sewing, and meal planning are very helpful, as are courses that focus on family living and home nursing.

Postsecondary Training

Most agencies will offer free training to prospective employees. Such training may include instruction on how to deal with depressed or reluctant patients, how to prepare easy and nutritious meals, and tips on housekeeping. Specific course work on health and sanitation may also be required.

Home health care aides must be willing to follow instructions and abide by the health plan created for each patient. Aides provide an important outreach service, supporting the care administered by the patient's physician, therapist, or social worker. They are not trained medical personnel, however, and must know the limits of their authority.

A Model Curriculum and Teaching Guide for the Instruction of the Homemaker-Home Health Aide was developed by the National HomeCaring Council. The training set forth in this curriculum combines classroom study and hands-on experience, with 60 hours of class instruction supplemented by an additional 15 hours of field work. It reflects the widespread desire to upgrade training for people in this field.

Health care agencies usually focus their training on first aid, hygiene, and the principles of health care. Cooking and nutrition, including meal preparation for patients with specific dietary needs, are often included in the program. Home health care aides may take courses in psychology and child development as well as family living. Because of the need for hands-on work, aides usually learn how to bathe, dress, and feed patients as well as how to help them walk upstairs or get up from bed. The more specific the skill required for certain patients, the more an agency is likely to have more comprehensive instruction.

The federal government has enacted guidelines for home health aides whose employers receive reimbursement from Medicare. Federal law requires home health aides to pass a competency test covering 12 areas: communication skills; observation, reporting, and documentation of patient status and the care or services furnished; reading and recording vital signs; basic infection control procedures; basic elements of body function and changes; maintenance of a clean, safe, and healthy environment; recognition of, and procedures for emergencies; physical, emotional, and developmental characteristics of the patients served; personal hygiene and grooming; safe transfer techniques; normal range of motion and positioning; and basic nutrition.

A home health care aide may also take training before taking the competency test. Federal law suggests at least 75 hours of classroom and practical training supervised by a registered nurse. Training and testing programs may be offered by the employing agency, but they must meet the standards of the Health Care Financing Administration. Training programs vary depending upon state regulations.

Certification or Licensing

The National Association for Home Care offers a National Homemaker-Home Health Aide certification. The certification is a voluntary demonstration that the individual has met industry standards.

Other Requirements

Caring for people in their own homes can be physically demanding work. Lifting a client for baths and exercise, helping a client up and down stairs, performing housework, and aiding with physical therapy all require that an aide be in good physical condition. Aides do not have the equipment and facilities of a hospital to help them with their work, and this requires adaptability and ingenuity. Oftentimes they must make do with the resources available in an average home.

An even temperament and a willingness to serve others are important characteristics for home health care aides. People in this occupation should be friendly, patient, sensitive to others' needs, and tactful. At times an aide will have to be stern in dealing with uncooperative patients or calm and understanding with those who are angry, confused, despondent, or in pain. Genuine warmth and respect for others are important attributes. Cheerfulness and a sense of humor can go a long way in establishing a good relationship with a client, and a good relationship can make working with the client much easier.

Exploring

Home health care aides are employed in many different areas. Interested students can learn more about the work by contacting local agencies and programs that provide home care services and requesting information on the organization's employment guidelines or training programs. Visiting the county or city health department and contacting the personnel director may provide useful information as well. Often, local organizations sponsor open houses to enlighten the community to the services they provide. This could serve as an excellent opportunity to meet the staff involved in hiring and program development and to learn about job opportunities. In addition, it may be possible to arrange to accompany a home health care aide on a home visit.

Employers

There are approximately 659,000 home health care aides employed in the United States. The primary employers of home health care aides are local social service agencies that provide home care services. Such agencies often have training programs for prospective employees. Home health care aides might also find employment with hospitals that operate their own community outreach programs. Most hospitals, however, hire home health care aides through agencies.

Starting Out

Some social service agencies enlist the aid of volunteers. By contacting agencies and inquiring about such openings, aspiring home care aides can get an introduction to the type of work this profession requires. Also, many agencies or nursing care facilities offer free training to prospective employees.

Checking the local Yellow Pages for agencies that provide health care to the aged and disabled or family-service organizations can provide a list of employment prospects. Nursing homes, public and private health care facilities, and local chapters of the Red Cross and United Way are likely to hire entry-level employees. The National HomeCaring Council can also supply information on reputable agencies and departments that employ home care aides.

Advancement

As home health care aides develop their skills and deepen their experience, they may advance to management or supervisory positions. Those who find greater enjoyment working with clients may branch into more specialized care and pursue additional training. Additional experience and education often bring higher pay and increased responsibility.

Aides who wish to work in a clinic or hospital setting may return to school to complete a nursing degree. Other related occupations include social worker, physical or occupational therapist, and dietitian. Along with a desire for advancement, however, must come the willingness to meet additional education and experience requirements.

Earnings

Earnings for home care aides are commensurate with salaries in related health care positions. Depending on the agency, considerable flexibility exists in working hours and patient load. For many aides who begin as part-time employees, the starting salary is usually the minimum hourly wage. For full-time aides with significant training or experience, earnings may be around $6 to $8 per hour. According to the U.S. Department of Labor, Medicare-certified aides earned an hourly average of $7.58 in 1998. Aides are usually paid only for the time worked in the home. They normally are not paid for travel time between jobs.

Work Environment

Health aides in a hospital or nursing home setting work at a much different pace and in a much different environment than the home health care aide. With home care, aides can take the time to sit with their clients and get to know them. Aides spend a certain amount of time with each client and can perform their responsibilities without the frequent distractions and demands of a hospital. Home surroundings differ from situation to situation. Some homes are neat and pleasant, while others are untidy and depressing. Some patients are angry, abusive, depressed, or otherwise difficult; others are pleasant and cooperative.

Because home health care aides usually have more than one patient, the hours an aide works can fluctuate based on the number of clients and types of services needed. Many clients may be ill or disabled. Some may be elderly and have no one else to assist them with light housekeeping or daily errands. These differences can dictate the type of responsibilities a home care aide has for each patient.

Vacation policies and benefits packages vary with the type and size of the employing agency. Many full-time home health care aides receive one week of paid vacation following their first year of employment, and they often receive two weeks of paid vacation each year thereafter. Full-time aides may also be eligible for health insurance and retirement benefits. Some agencies also offer holiday or overtime compensation.

Working with the infirm or disabled can be a rewarding experience as aides enhance the quality of their clients' lives with their help and company. However, the personal strains—on the clients as well as the aides—can make the work challenging and occasionally frustrating. There can be difficult emotional demands that aides may find exhausting. Considerable physical activity is involved in this line of work, such as helping patients to walk, dress, or take care of themselves. Traveling from one home to another and running various errands for patients can also be tiring and time-consuming, or it can be a pleasant break.

Outlook

As government and private agencies develop more programs to assist the dependent, the need for home health care aides will continue to grow. Because of the physical and emotional demands of the job, there is high turnover and, therefore, frequent job openings for home health care aides.

Also, the number of people 70 years of age and older is expected to increase substantially, and many of them will require at least some home care. Rising health care costs are causing many insurance companies to consider alternatives to hospital treatment, so many insurance providers now cover home care services. In addition, hospitals and nursing homes are trying to balance the demand for their services and their limitations in staff and physical facilities. The availability of home health care aides can allow such institutions as hospitals and nursing homes to offer quality care to more people.

For More Information

For information about a career as a home health care aide and schools offering training, contact the following organizations:

National Association of Health Career Schools
750 First Street, NE, Suite 940
Washington, DC 20002
Tel: 202-842-1592
Email: nahcs@aol.com
Web: http://www.nahcs.org/

National Association for Home Care
228 Seventh Street, SE
Washington, DC 20003
Tel: 202-547-7424
Web: http://www.nahc.org

Human Services Workers

School Subjects
Health
Sociology

Personal Skills
Communication/ideas
Helping/teaching

Work Environment
Primarily indoors
Primarily one location

Minimum Education Level
Some postsecondary training

Salary Range
$13,500 to $21,300 to $33,800

Certification or Licensing
None available

Outlook
Much faster than the average

Overview

Under the supervision of social workers, psychologists, sociologists, and other professionals, *human services workers* offer support to families, the elderly, the poor, and others in need. They teach life and communication skills to people in mental health facilities or substance abuse programs. Employed by agencies, shelters, halfway houses, and hospitals, they work individually with clients or in group counseling. They also direct clients to social services and benefits. There are approximately 268,000 human services workers employed in the United States.

History

Before the 20th century, charity and philanthropy consisted mainly of donations from the affluent. These donations were distributed by church groups to the needy. No systematic methods were established to follow up on charity cases or improve the conditions of the poor in any permanent way.

After the Industrial Revolution, public opinion about the inequities of wealth began to change. In 1889, Jane Addams, the daughter of a banker, founded Hull House in Chicago, an act that is usually considered the birth of formal social work. Addams's philosophy of helping the underprivileged gain a better, more permanent standard of living inspired many others to launch similar programs in other parts of the world. After World War I, social work began to be recognized as a valid career. The Great Depression of the 1930s provided further impetus to the growth of social work, as the federal government joined with state, municipal, and private efforts to ease the pain of poverty. The social disruptions of the years following World War II contributed to further growth in social work. Today, social workers and human services workers are employed in a variety of institutional and community settings, administering help and support to the poor, the homeless, the aged, the disabled and mentally ill, substance abusers, parolees, and others having trouble with adjustments in life.

The Job

A group of teenagers in a large high school are concerned about the violence that threatens them every day. They have seen their friends and classmates hurt in the school's hallways, on the basketball court, and in the parking lot. In a place built for their education, they fear for their safety, and each of them has something to say about it. They have something to say to the administration, to the parents, and, most of all, to the kids who carry guns and knives to school. Human services workers come to their aid. Human services workers step in to support the efforts of social workers, psychologists, and other professional agencies or programs. Human services workers may work in a school, a community center, a housing project, or a hospital. They may work as aides, assistants, technicians, or counselors. In the case of the high school students who want to improve conditions in their school, human services workers serve as group leaders under the supervision of a school social worker, meeting with some of the students to discuss their fears and concerns. They also meet with administrators, faculty, and parents. Eventually, they conduct a school-wide series of group discussions—listening, taking notes, offering advice, and most important, empowering people to better their communities and their lives.

The term "human services" covers a wide range of careers, from counseling prison inmates to counseling the families of murder victims; from helping someone with a disability find a job to caring for the child of a teenage mother during the school day. From one-on-one interaction to group interaction, from paperwork to footwork, the human services worker is focused on improving the lives of others.

As society changes, so do the concerns of human services workers. New societal problems (such as the rapid spread of AIDS among teenagers and the threat of gang violence) require special attention, as do changes in the population (such as the increasing number of elderly people living on their own and the increasing number of minimum-wage workers unable to fully provide for their families). New laws and political movements also affect human services workers because many social service programs rely heavily on federal and state aid. Although government policy makers are better educated than the policy makers of years past, social service programs are more threatened than ever before. Despite all these changes in society and the changes in the theories of social work, some things stay the same—human services workers care about the well-being of individuals and communities. They are sensitive to the needs of diverse groups of people, and they are actively involved in meeting the needs of the public.

Human services workers have had many of the same responsibilities throughout the years. They offer their clients counseling, representation, emotional support, and the services they need. Although some human services workers assist professionals with the development and evaluation of social programs, policy analysis, and other administrative duties, most work directly with clients.

This direct work can involve aid to specific populations, such as ethnic groups, women, and the poor. Many human services workers assist poor people in numerous ways. They interview clients to identify needed services. They care for clients' children during job or medical appointments and offer clients emotional support. They determine whether clients are eligible for food stamps, Medicaid, or other welfare programs. In some food stamp programs, aides advise low-income family members how to plan, budget, shop for, and prepare balanced meals, often accompanying or driving clients to the store and offering suggestions on the most nutritious and economical food to purchase.

Some aides serve tenants in public housing projects. They are employed by housing agencies or other groups to help tenants relocate. They inform tenants of the use of facilities and the location of community services, such as recreation centers and clinics. They also explain the management's rules about sanitation and maintenance. They may at times help resolve disagreements between tenants and landlords.

Members of specific populations call on the aid of human services workers for support, information, and representation. The human services worker can provide these clients with counseling and emotional support and direct them to support groups and services. Social workers work with human services workers to reach out to the people; together, they visit individuals, families, and neighborhood groups to publicize the supportive services available.

Other clients of human services workers are those experiencing life-cycle changes. Children, adolescents, and the elderly may require assistance in making transitions. Human services workers help parents find proper day care for their children. They educate young mothers in how to care for an infant. They counsel children struggling with family problems or peer pressure. They offer emotional support to gay, lesbian, and bisexual teenagers and involve them in support groups. Some programs help the elderly stay active and help them prepare meals and clean their homes. They also assist the elderly in getting to and from hospitals and community centers and stay in touch with these clients through home visits and telephone calls.

Some human services workers focus on specific problems, such as drug and alcohol abuse. Human services workers assist in developing, organizing, and conducting programs dealing with the causes of and remedies for substance abuse. Workers may help individuals trying to overcome drug or alcohol addiction to master practical skills, such as cooking and doing laundry, and teach them ways to communicate more effectively with others. Domestic violence is also a problem receiving more attention, as more and more people leave abusive situations. Shelters for victims require counselors, assistants, tutors, and day care personnel for their children. Human services workers may also teach living and communication skills in homeless shelters and mental health facilities.

Record keeping is an important part of the duties of human services workers, since records may affect a client's eligibility for future benefits, the proper assessment of a program's success, and the prospect of future funding. Workers prepare and maintain records and case files of every person with whom they work. They record clients' responses to the various programs and treatment. They must also track costs in group homes in order to stay within budget.

Requirements

High School

Some employers will hire people with only a high school education, but these employees might find it hard to move beyond clerical positions. Interested high school students should plan to attend a college or university and should take classes in English, mathematics, political science, psychology, and sociology.

Postsecondary Training

Certificate and associate's degree programs in human services or mental health are offered at community and junior colleges, vocational-technical institutes, and other postsecondary institutions. It is also possible to pursue a bachelor's degree in human services. Almost 500 human services education programs exist; academic programs such as these prepare students for occupations in the human services. Because the educators at these colleges and universities stay in regular contact with the social work employers in their area, the programs are continually revised to meet the changing needs of the field. Students are exposed early and often to the kinds of situations they may encounter on the job.

Undergraduate and graduate programs typically include courses in psychology, sociology, crisis intervention, family dynamics, therapeutic interviewing, rehabilitation, and gerontology.

Other Requirements

Many people perform human services work because they want to make a difference in their community. They may also like connecting on a personal level with other people, offering them emotional support, helping them sort out problems, and teaching them how to care for themselves and their families. A genuine interest in the lives and concerns of others and a sensitivity to their situations is important to a human services worker. An artistic background can also be valuable in human services. Some programs in mental health facilities, domestic violence shelters, and other group homes use art therapy. Painting, music, dance, and creative writing are sometimes incorporated into counseling sessions, providing a client with alternative modes of expression.

In addition to the rewarding aspects of the job, a human services worker must be prepared to take on difficult responsibilities. The work can be very stressful. The problems of some populations—such as prison inmates, battered women and children, substance abusers, and the poor—can seem insurmountable. Their stories and day-to-day lives can seem tragic. Even if human services workers are not counseling clients, they are working directly with clients on some level. Just helping a person fill out an application or prepare a household budget requires a good disposition and the ability to be supportive. Clients may not welcome help and may not even care about their own well-being. In these cases, a human services worker must remain firm but supportive and encouraging. Patience is very important, whatever the area of human service.

The workload for a human services worker can also be overwhelming. An agency with limited funding cannot always afford to hire the number of employees it needs. A human services worker employed by an understaffed agency will probably be overworked. This can sometimes result in employee burnout.

Employers

Human services workers are employed in a variety of settings, including agency offices, community centers, group homes, halfway houses, mental health facilities, hospitals, shelters, and the private homes of clients.

Exploring

To get an idea of the requirements of human service, you can volunteer your time to a local human services agency or institution. Church organizations also involve young people in volunteer work, as do the Red Cross, the Boy Scouts, and the Girl Scouts. Volunteer work could include reading to blind or elderly people and visiting nursing homes and halfway homes. You might get involved organizing group recreation programs at the YMCA or YWCA or performing light clerical duties in an office. You could also encourage any high school organizations to which you belong to become actively involved in charity work.

Some members of high school organizations also perform social services within their own schools, educating classmates on the dangers of gangs, unsafe sex, and substance abuse. By being actively involved in your community, you can gain experience in human services as well as build up a history of volunteer service that will impress future employers.

Starting Out

Students may find jobs through their high school counselors or local and state human services agencies. Sometimes summer jobs and volunteer work can develop into full-time employment upon graduation. Employers try to be selective in their hiring because many human services jobs involve direct contact with people who are impaired and therefore vulnerable to exploitation. Evidence of helping others is a definite advantage.

Advancement

Job performance has some bearing on pay raises and advancement for human services workers. However, career advancement almost always depends on formal education, such as a bachelor's or master's degree in social work, counseling, rehabilitation, or some other related field. Many employers encourage their workers to further their education, and some may even reimburse part of the costs of school. In addition, many employers provide in-service training, such as seminars and workshops.

Earnings

Salaries of human services workers depend in part on their employer and amount of experience. According to the *Occupational Outlook Handbook,* starting salaries for human services workers average about $21,300 year. The lowest paid human services workers earned less than $13,500. Experienced workers can earn more than $33,800 annually.

Work Environment

Most human services workers work a standard 40-hour week, spending time both in the office and in the field interviewing clients and performing other support services. Some weekend and evening work may be required, but compensatory time off is usually granted. Workers in residential settings generally work in shifts. Because group homes need 24-hour staffing, workers usually work some evenings and weekends.

Work conditions are affected by the size and location of the town in which the work is found. The societal problems of large, urban areas are different from those of small, rural areas. In a city, human services workers deal with issues of crime, racism, gang warfare, and violence in the schools. These problems can exist in smaller communities as well, but the human services workers of rural areas focus more on work with the elderly and the poor. Rural communities typically have an older population, with people living deeper in the country and farther from public and private services. This can require more transportation time. The social services in rural areas, because of lower salaries and poorer facilities, typically have trouble attracting workers.

Offices and facilities may be clean and cheerful, or they may be dismal, cramped, and inadequately equipped. While out in the field with clients, workers may also find themselves in dangerous, squalid areas. In a large city, workers can rely on public transportation, whereas workers in a rural community must often drive long distances.

Outlook

Employment for human services workers will grow much faster than the average through 2008, according to the U.S. Department of Labor. Much of this growth is expected to occur in homes for the mentally impaired and developmentally disabled. Also, the life expectancy for people in the United States continues to rise, requiring more assistance for the elderly, such as adult day care and meal delivery. Correctional facilities are also expected to employ many more human services workers. Because counseling inmates and offenders can be undesirable work, there are a number of high-paying jobs available in that area.

New ideas in treating disabled or mentally ill people also influence employment growth in group homes and residential care facilities. Public concern for the homeless—many of whom are former mental patients who were released under service reductions in the 1980s—as well as troubled teenagers, and those with substance abuse problems, is likely to bring about new community-based programs and group residences.

Job prospects in public agencies are not as bright as they once were because of fiscal policies that tighten eligibility requirements for federal welfare and other payments. State and local governments are expected to remain major employers, however, as the burden of providing social services such as welfare, child support, and nutrition programs is shifted from the federal government to the state and local level. In larger cities, such as New York or Washington, DC, jobs in the public sector will be more plentiful than in a smaller city because of the higher demand. There is also a higher burnout rate in the larger cities, resulting in more job opportunities as people vacate their positions for other careers.

For More Information

For more information on careers in counseling, contact:

American Counseling Association
5999 Stevenson Avenue
Alexandria, VA 22304-3300
Tel: 800-347-6647
Web: http://www.counseling.org/

For information on student memberships, scholarships, and the online career pamphlet, **The Human Services Worker,** *check out the following Web site:*

National Organization for Human Service Education
Web: http://www.nohse.com/

Nonprofit Social Service Directors

	School Subjects
Government Psychology Sociology	
	Personal Skills
Helping/teaching Leadership/management	
	Work Environment
Primarily indoors Primarily one location	
	Minimum Education Level
Bachelor's degree	
	Salary Range
$65,960 to $75,000 to $100,000+	
	Certification or Licensing
Required by all states	
	Outlook
Much faster than the average	

Overview

Nonprofit social service directors, also known as *nonprofit directors, nonprofit chief executive officers,* or *nonprofit administrators,* are at the top rung on the agency's ladder. No matter what area the agency specializes in—health care, services for the aging, or youth development, for example—the director is the individual who spearheads the organization's efforts, operations, and progress. A director's duties may include hiring and managing staff, fundraising, budgeting, public relations, and, depending on the agency, working directly with the clientele served.

History

Social service organizations have been around in various forms for hundreds of years. During the Middle Ages, organizations formed to care for the sick and the poor. By the 1800s, the Industrial Revolution was changing society's structure as numerous people moved from small towns and farms to cities where they worked in industries and had few, if any, established social support systems. The cities became more crowded, wages were low, and life became more complicated. After the Civil War, there was an explosion of social service organizations—groups caring for the sick and the poor, and, increasingly, for immigrants. Under President Roosevelt's administration during the 1930s, many "new deal" programs, such as unemployment insurance, were established to help people deal with the effects of the Depression. During the 1960s, President Johnson's administration followed a similar agenda of promoting the well-being of all citizens with the "Great Society" programs, such as Medicare. These programs increased the role of the government in the welfare of individuals and stimulated the growth of private social service organizations. In the years that followed, the older organizations expanded and many new organizations emerged.

By the end of the 20th century, however, social support systems had begun to change. The federal government, responding to the unpopularity of the expense of many government social service programs, eliminated some programs and cut back on many others. Perhaps the best-known cutback was the Welfare Reform Bill, which was designed to shorten the length of time welfare recipients receive benefits. Reforms at the national level mean that state governments often find themselves trying to provide money to keep programs running. If the funds can't be found at the state level, the slack may be picked up at the city level. If the city is unable to come up with the necessary funds, the services usually pass out of the hands of governmental officials altogether and into the hands of local or national nonprofit organizations.

The need for nongovernmental organizations to fill in gaps left by federal, state, and local programs has changed the profile of charity work. Where many organizations once had untrained volunteers, they now often require trained, full-time staff. As nonprofit social service work has become more crucial to national infrastructure, nonprofits have become increasingly professional. Nonprofit organizations are dependent on intelligent, educated, and savvy direction in order to work. Fund-raising, budgeting, resource management, and public relations are just a few areas where top-notch business skills are a necessity. The role of those who run the organizations—administrators, executive directors, and directors —is crucial.

The Job

Anyone looking for a career that provides a diversity of responsibilities, satisfaction, meaning, action, and a wide realm of options should certainly consider entering the field of social work. *Social workers* are people who are committed to making a positive difference in the human condition, and the director of an organization has the primary responsibility of seeing that the organization achieves its goals and impacts positively on the lives of the people it's designed to serve.

An aspect of social work that sets it apart from other helping professions is the concept of helping people in their environments. Social workers help clients not only with how they feel about a situation, but also with what they can do about it. For example, a woman suffering stress from being a single parent may be referred by a social worker to a child care agency. The social worker also might help her explore other options, such as getting flextime at work. In addition, the social worker might provide therapy or counseling or refer the client to a qualified therapist for assistance in managing her stress. A wide variety of nonprofit organizations are at work in the United States today, and each has a different mission and set of services.

Because it now takes such a high level of professional sophistication to keep a nonprofit going, directing these sorts of organizations is becoming a complex, challenging, and varied career. At one time, the biggest prerequisite to those who wanted to work in social services was a big heart. Today, compassion is still a necessary quality to have, but knowledge, skill, and talent are just as important. A director of a social services organization may be in charge of managing staff, overseeing the budget, spearheading fund-raising efforts, and handling public relations issues.

Sheri Flanigan served for three years as the Executive Director of La Casa Latina, Inc., a nonprofit organization with the mission to "empower the Latino population to become part of the Siouxland community." Flanigan says about her work, "There was no 'typical day.' I spent about half of my time on administration: budgeting, fund-raising, grant writing, staff supervision, community meetings, and board meetings. Because we were small (five staff members and a $150,000 budget), I did all of the bookkeeping and payroll. The other half of my time, I provided direct services—translations and interpretation primarily. I also filled in when another staff member was out."

Flanigan notes that the diversity of her experiences was one of the best parts of the job. Because she worked for a small organization, she could work on both a macro and a micro level. She was able to see the fruits of her organization's labors on a community-wide level, but she also enjoyed the time she was able to spend working directly with the agency's clients.

In any nonprofit organization, even as the top individual in the structure, the nature of a director's work likely will be determined largely by a board of directors. This board, plus the size and nature of the organization, will define the director's duties to a large extent.

Requirements

High School

If you're interested in nonprofit social services work, you'll want to concentrate on humanities and social science courses such as English, history, government, sociology, and psychology. Such courses will give you perspective on the issues confronting the people that a nonprofit organization will be trying to help. Communication skills are critical, so in addition to English, take public speaking courses to hone your skills. The ability to speak a foreign language will be a big plus in many organizations; consider taking Spanish, as it is the second most common language spoken in this country. At the director level of a nonprofit agency, you will be responsible for budget expenditures; therefore, you should have mathematics and accounting knowledge, so be sure to include these classes in your schedule. Finally, take computer science courses so that you will be able to use the computer for activities such as creating budgets, writing grant proposals, and keeping a database of information on clients.

Postsecondary Training

Most nonprofit social service organizations will require that you have a degree in social work from a college or university program accredited by the Council on Social Work Education. The undergraduate degree is the Bachelor of Social Work (B.S.W.). Graduate degrees include the Master of Social Work (M.S.W.) and the Doctorate in Social Work (D.S.W.) or Ph.D. The undergraduate degree will allow you to find entry-level positions at many agencies. Typical courses of study for the B.S.W. include classes in social welfare policies, human behavior and the social environment, research methods, and ethics. In addition, accredited programs require you to complete at least 400 hours of supervised field experience. To advance to the level of director, you will need to have a master's or doctorate degree.

Obtaining an M.S.W. degree usually requires two years of courses, along with 900 hours of supervised fieldwork. You may be able to enter a master's program without having a B.S.W.; however, you should have a background that includes psychology, sociology, biology, economics, and social work courses.

Certification or Licensing

According to the U.S. Department of Labor, all states have some type of licensing, certification, or registration requirement for those practicing social work and using professional titles. However, the standards and requirements vary from state to state, and those wanting to work as social workers will need to check with their state licensing boards. These licensing, certification, or registration requirements may or may not be necessary for the director, depending on the nature of the organization and the duties of the director. Again, those wanting to work as directors will need to contact the regulatory board of the state in which they want to work to find out specific requirements. The American Association of State Social Work Boards may also be able to provide such information (see the end of this article for contact information).

Other Requirements

It takes a certain kind of person to succeed in social services. According to Sheri Flanigan, "you can't be afraid to 'touch' low-income people. From my experiences, I find that even the most well-meaning people have difficulty working in this field if they are uncomfortable interacting with the clientele. In addition, social services are notoriously understaffed, so you also have to be willing to do the work (answer the phone, make copies, etc). Even though you shouldn't be doing these things for a large portion of the day as a director, you have to be willing to work side by side with the other staff." Social services workers and directors also need to be emotionally stable, objective about situations they face, and responsible.

Exploring

The best way of exploring this field is by doing volunteer work for a nonprofit social service organization such as a hospice, shelter, or community outreach organization. Volunteering will give you exposure to the work environment as well as the situations an organization's clients face and help you develop your listening and communications skills. It can also give you an understanding of the way nonprofits work and the kind of expectations employers will have.

Flanigan agrees and says, "Volunteer at a variety of social service organizations. This will give you the opportunity to see close-up how these types of organizations function and to evaluate the pros and the cons. The experience will also look good on a resume."

Employers

Nonprofit social service organizations vary in size, purpose, and location. There are large, national nonprofit youth advocacy agencies in the thick of policy issues in Washington, DC, for example. On the other hand, there are hospices, shelters, and youth support centers in small, community-oriented settings. The nature of the work a director does may also vary, depending on the organization and its size, needs, goals, and board of directors. For example, some social welfare nonprofits focus on changing legislation or public perceptions of certain social issues. These organizations will work differently from those that focus more on working directly with those needing services.

Starting Out

With your B.S.W. or M.S.W. in hand, you should be able to find entry-level work in the social services field. Your college placement office will have contacts to get you started, and the contacts you've made through your professors and colleagues will be invaluable in referring you to vacant positions.

Many social service directors started their careers as volunteers, then, as employees, worked their way up the ranks. Sheri Flanigan entered the field as a Volunteer to Service in America (VISTA) volunteer. "VISTA was an excellent way for me to become familiar with the social service organization without having to start at entry level. I believe that service corp is what you make of it. It is easy as a volunteer not to put a lot of effort into the job, but don't fall into that trap. It is an excellent time to explore your opportunities, and to put a lot of effort into making your project work."

Advancement

As the director or executive director of an organization, it can be difficult to see advancement opportunities because these people are already at the top levels of their organizations. A director, however, may see advancement as broadening the goals of his or her organization, increasing funding, or raising public awareness about the issues the organization addresses. Directors can also advance by moving from one nonprofit to another, larger nonprofit agency. Flanigan has a recommendation: "Look to grow your organization. You start as the executive director of a small nonprofit organization and soon you're the executive director of a large nonprofit—an organization that you nurtured and grew. There is also the possibility of being hired at a larger organization or an organization more tailored to your interests."

Earnings

Salaries in nonprofit work are typically lower than those paid for comparable work in the for-profit sector. In addition, salaries in the nonprofit sector vary tremendously depending on the size, location, and purpose of the organization. Large, high-profile nonprofits with specialized staff and budgets in the millions of dollars, for example, may pay directors well over $100,000, but six-figure salaries are still the exception in this field. A 1998 survey by *The NonProfit Times* found that chief executives, or directors, working for large foundations had the highest yearly earnings, averaging approximately $103,980, while those working for social or welfare agencies had the lowest yearly earnings, averaging approximately $65,960. According to a 2000 salary survey published by Abbott, Langer & Associates, Inc., the median annual income for chief executive officers of nonprofits was $75,000. It is important to keep in mind that the director job is an advanced position. Those just starting out in the field will earn much less. For example, the U.S. Department of Labor reports that social workers had a median annual income of $30,590 in 1998. People in this field, however, find that they have the reward of emotional satisfaction not found in every job.

Nonprofit organizations often offer benefits packages that can't be beat. In most agencies, employees can expect liberal annual paid vacation days, generous sick leave, health and hospitalization insurance, retirement plans, and good personnel practices.

Work Environment

Many social services directors feel this emotional satisfaction to be the best part of the job. In addition to the emotional benefits gained from working directly with clients, there are also the benefits from close relationships with colleagues. Nonprofits make great employers because of the positive work environment that they promote; nonprofits are typically humanitarian, responsive to stress, and supportive emotionally. However, these organizations almost always are run on tight budgets, and directors may have to deal with the constant threat of cutbacks or even closure. This can be stressful, and the director must concentrate on the "business" aspect of the work by getting funding, keeping costs down, and meeting with legislators or potential donors. Directors interact with many different people throughout their workdays and must be able to handle a variety of social situations. The tone of the work environment—dedicated, creative, community-oriented—is often set by the director's actions. Working hard and long hours promotes commitment to the job by everyone.

Outlook

The need for social service agencies is expected to increase markedly through 2008. The expected rapid growth is due to expanding services for the elderly, the mentally and physically disabled, and families in crisis. Our nation's elderly comprise a rapidly expanding segment of the population that is likely to need a wide range of social services. The growing emphasis on providing home care services, enabling aging seniors to remain at home rather than relocate to costly skilled nursing facilities, will contribute to employment growth in the social services industry. A continuing influx of foreign-born nationals to this country will spur the demand for a range of social services, such as financial, relocation, and job training assistance. Child protective services and special groups, such as adults who were abused as children, are also on the rise. In addition, crime, juvenile delinquency, mental illness, developmental disabilities, AIDS, and individual and family crises will spur demand for social services. Every agency will need to be overseen by a capable and savvy director. Many job openings will also stem from the need to replace nonprofit social service directors who leave their posts. The need for top level executives and directors is projected to increase by 37.9 percent by 2008, according to the U.S. Bureau of Labor Statistics.

For More Information

This alliance of colleges, universities, and nonprofit organizations prepares undergraduates for careers with youth and human services agencies. For more information, contact:

American Humanics
4601 Madison Avenue
Kansas City, MO 64112
Tel: 816-561-6415
Email: info@humanics.org
Web: http://www.humanics.org

For a list of regulatory agencies or for a comparison of state regulations regarding licensing, certification, and registration, contact:

Association of Social Work Boards
400 South Ridge Parkway, Suite B
Culpeper, VA 22701
Tel: 800-225-6880
Email: info@aswb
Web: http://www.aasswb.org

For information on social work careers and educational programs, contact:

Council on Social Work Education
1725 Duke Street, Suite 500
Alexandria, VA 22314
Tel: 703-683-8080
Email: info@cswe.org
Web: http://www.cswe.org

To access the online publication, Choices: Careers in Social Work, *check out the* NASW *Web site:*

National Association of Social Workers (NASW)
750 First Street, NE, Suite 700
Washington DC 20002-4241
Tel: 800-638-8799
Web: http://www.naswdc.org

For information on student memberships, scholarships, and the online career pamphlet, The Human Services Worker, *check out the following Web site:*

National Organization for Human Service Education
Web: http://www.nohse.com

For information on volunteer opportunities, visit the following Web site:

VISTA (Volunteers In Service To America)
Web: http://www.friendsofvista.org

Occupational Therapists

	School Subjects
Biology Health	
	Personal Skills
Helping/teaching Mechanical/manipulative	
	Work Environment
Primarily indoors Primarily one location	
	Minimum Education Level
Bachelor's degree	
	Salary Range
$30,850 to $48,230 to $86,540+	
	Certification or Licensing
Required by all states	
	Outlook
Faster than the average	

Overview

Occupational therapists select and direct therapeutic activities designed to develop or restore maximum function to individuals with disabilities. There are approximately 73,000 occupational therapists employed in the United States.

History

Since about the 14th century, physicians have recognized the therapeutic value of providing activities and occupations for their patients. Observations that mental patients tended to recover more quickly from their illnesses led physicians to involve their patients in such activities as agriculture, weaving, working with animals, and sewing. Over time, this practice became quite common, and the conditions of many patients were improved.

Occupational therapy as we know it today had its beginning after World War I. The need to help disabled veterans of that war, and years later the veterans of World War II, stimulated its growth. Even though its inception was in the psychiatric field, occupational therapy has developed an equally important role in other medical fields, including rehabilitation of physically disabled patients.

Traditionally, occupational therapists taught creative arts such as weaving, clay modeling, leather work, jewelry making, and other crafts to promote their patients' functional skills. Today, occupational therapists focus more on providing activities that are designed to promote skills needed in daily living, including self-care; employment education and job skills, such as typing, the operation of computers and computer programs, or the use of power tools; and community and social skills.

It is important to note the difference between occupational therapists and *physical therapists*. Physical therapy is chiefly concerned with helping people with physical disabilities or injuries to regain functions, or adapt to or overcome their physical limitations. Occupational therapists work with physical factors, but also the psychological and social elements of their clients' disabilities, helping them become as independent as possible in the home, school, and workplace. Occupational therapists work not only with the physically challenged, but with people with mental and emotional disabilities as well.

The Job

Occupational therapists use a wide variety of activities to help clients attain their goals for productive, independent living. These goals include developing maximum self-sufficiency in activities of daily living, such as eating, dressing, writing, using a telephone and other communication resources, as well as functioning in the community and the workplace.

In developing a therapeutic program for a client, the occupational therapist often works as a member of a team that can include physicians, nurses, psychiatrists, physical therapists, speech therapists, rehabilitation counselors, social workers, and other specialists. Occupational therapists use creative, educational, and recreational activities, as well as human ingenuity, in helping people achieve their full potential, regardless of their disabilities. Each therapy program is designed specifically for the individual client.

Occupational therapists help clients explore their likes and dislikes, their abilities, and their creative, educational, and recreational experiences. Therapists help people choose activities that have the most appeal and value for them. For example, an activity may be designed to promote greater dexterity for someone with arthritic fingers. Learning to use an adapted computer might help a young person with a spinal cord injury to succeed in school and career goals. The therapist works with the clients' interests and helps them develop practical skills and functional independence.

The occupational therapist may work with a wide range of clients. They may assist a client in learning to use an artificial limb. Another client may have suffered a stroke or other neurological disability, and the therapist works with the client to redevelop their motor functions or reeducate their muscle function. Therapists may assist in the growth and development of premature infants, or they may work with disabled children, helping them learn motor skills or develop skills and tools that will aid them in their education and social interaction.

Some therapists also conduct research to develop new types of therapies and activities and to measure the effectiveness of a therapy program. They may also design and make special equipment or splints to help clients perform their activities.

Other duties may include supervision of volunteer workers, student therapists, and occupational therapy assistants who give instruction in a particular skill. Therapists must prepare reports to keep members of the professional team informed.

Chief occupational therapists in a hospital may teach medical and nursing students the principles of occupational therapy. Many occupational therapists have administrative duties such as directing different kinds of occupational therapy programs, coordinating patient activities, and acting as consultants or advisors to local and state health departments, mental health authorities, and the Division of Vocational Rehabilitation.

Requirements

High School

Since occupational therapists require a college degree, taking college preparatory classes in high school is a must for anyone interested in this career. Courses such as biology, chemistry, and health will expose you to the science fields. Other courses, such as art and social sciences, will help give you an understanding of other aspects of your future work. Also important is a strong background in English. Remember, occupational therapy is a career oriented towards helping people. To be able to work with many different people with different needs, you will need excellent communication skills. Also, keep in mind that college admission officers will look favorably at any experience you have had working in the health care field, either in volunteer or paid positions.

Postsecondary Training

Preparation for occupational therapy requires the completion of an accredited program in occupational therapy, either at the bachelor's or master's degree level. More than 100 colleges and universities offer occupational therapy programs that have been accredited by the Council on Medical Education and Hospitals of the American Medical Association and the American Occupational Therapy Association.

College preparation for occupational therapy emphasizes biological and behavioral sciences. Courses include anatomy, physiology, neurology, psychology, human growth and development, and sociology. Clinical subjects cover general medical and surgical conditions, and interpretation of the principles and practice of occupational therapy in pediatrics, psychiatry, orthopedics, general medicine, and surgery. Many bachelor's degree programs require students to fulfill two years of general study before specializing in occupational therapy during the last two years.

Graduates of a bachelor's degree program in occupational therapy are required to undergo a six-month clinical training period in order to qualify for professional registration. The armed forces also offers programs whereby graduates of approved schools of occupational therapy who meet the requirements to become commissioned officers may receive the clinical part of their training while in the service.

College graduates with training in other fields may apply for entry into a master's program or a certificate program. These advanced programs generally last from two to two-and-a-half years and include both academic and clinical work.

Occupational therapists with bachelor's degrees may decide to continue their education in an advanced degree program. Master's and doctoral programs are advised for occupational therapists seeking careers in teaching, administration, and research.

In addition to these full-time study options, there are a limited number of part-time and evening programs that allow prospective occupational therapists to work in another field while completing their requirements in occupational therapy.

Certification or Licensing

Upon graduation and completion of the clinical practice period, therapists are eligible to take the examination administered by the American Occupational Therapy Certification Board. Those who pass this examination may use the initials OTR (Occupational Therapist, Registered) after their names. Many hospitals require that their occupational therapists be registered. A license to practice occupational therapy is required by all states and the District of Columbia. Applicants for a license must have a degree or certificate from an accredited educational program and pass the national certification examination.

Other Requirements

Occupational therapists should enjoy working with people. They should have a patient, calm, and compassionate temperament and have the ability to encourage and inspire their clients.

Exploring

While in high school, students interested in a career in occupational therapy should meet with occupational therapists, visit the facilities where they work, and gain an understanding of the types of equipment and skills they use. Many hospitals and occupational therapy facilities and departments also have volunteer opportunities, which will give students strong insight into this career.

Employers

There are approximately 73,000 occupational therapists at work in hospitals, schools, nursing homes, home health agencies, mental health centers, adult day care programs, outpatient clinics, and residential care facilities. A growing number are self-employed, in either solo or group practice or in consulting firms.

Starting Out

A school's placement office is usually the best place to start a job search for a newly graduated occupational therapist. Individuals may also apply directly to government agencies, such as the U.S. Public Health Service, private hospitals, and clinics. In addition, the American Occupational Therapy Association can provide job seekers with assistance through its employment bulletins.

Advancement

Newly graduated occupational therapists usually begin as staff therapists and may qualify as senior therapists after several years on the job. The Army, Navy, Air Force, and the U.S. Public Health Service commission occupational therapists; other branches of the federal service give civil service ratings. Experienced therapists may become directors of occupational therapy programs in large hospitals, clinics, or workshops or they may become teachers. Some positions are available as program coordinators and as consultants with large institutions and agencies.

A few colleges and health agencies offer advanced courses in the treatment of special disabilities, such as those resulting from cerebral palsy. Some institutions provide in-service programs for therapists.

Earnings

According to the U.S. Department of Labor, salaries for occupational therapists in 1998 averaged about $48,230. The lowest 10 percent earned $30,850 a year; the top 10 percent earned more than $86,540. Administrators earn an average of $55,000 per year.

Salaries for occupational therapists often vary according to where they work. In areas where the cost of living is higher, occupational therapists generally receive higher pay. Occupational therapists employed in public schools earn salaries that vary by school district. In some states, they are classified as teachers and are paid accordingly.

Therapists employed at hospitals, and government and public agencies generally receive full benefit packages that include vacation and sick pay, health insurance, and retirement benefits. Self-employed therapists and those who run their own businesses must provide their own benefits.

Work Environment

Occupational therapists work in occupational therapy workshops or clinics. Such places are usually well-lighted, pleasant settings. Generally, they work an eight-hour day, 40-hour week, with some evening work required in a few organizations.

Outlook

Opportunities for occupational therapists are expected to be highly favorable through 2008 and will grow faster than the average for all other careers. This growth will occur as a result of the increasing number of middle-aged and elderly people that require therapeutic services. The demand for occupational therapists is also increasing because of growing public interest in and government support for people with disabilities and for occupational therapy programs helping people attain the fullest possible functional status. The demand for rehabilitative and long-term care services is expected to grow strongly over the next decade. There will be numerous opportunities for work with mental health clients, children, and the elderly, as well as with those with disabling conditions.

As the health care industry continues to be restructured, there should be many more opportunities for occupational therapists in nontraditional settings. This factor and proposed changes in the laws should create an excellent climate for therapists wishing to enter private practice. Home health care may experience the greatest growth in the next decade.

For More Information

For further information on a career in occupational therapy, contact:

American Occupational Therapy Association
4720 Montgomery Lane
PO Box 31220
Bethesda, MD 20824-1220
Tel: 301-652-2682
Web: http://www.aota.org

For information on certification requirements, contact:

American Occupational Therapy Certification Board
1383 Piccard Drive, Suite 300
Rockville, MD 20851
Tel: 301-990-7979

Orientation and Mobility Specialists

Health Psychology	School Subjects
Communication/ideas Helping/teaching	Personal Skills
Primarily indoors Primarily multiple locations	Work Environment
Bachelor's degree	Minimum Education Level
$19,250 to $30,590 to $49,080	Salary Range
Required by certain states	Certification or Licensing
Faster than the average	Outlook

Overview

Orientation and mobility specialists help people with disabilities stay actively involved in society. They teach blind, visually impaired, and disabled individuals how to master the skills necessary to live independently, and may encourage them to participate in various educational or recreational programs. Specialists also serve as a source of information, referring clients to financial aid, benefits, and legal advice. These workers may be employed directly by an individual or indirectly through community planning, research, and publicity projects.

History

Helping those with disabilities has long been a part of the social work profession. As early as 1657, facilities called almshouses provided shelter, food, and work to the poor and those with disabilities. In the mid-1800s, middle-class women referred to as "friendly visitors" visited the homes of poor families to instruct the disabled in household management, the pursuit of employment, and the education of children. However, these friendly visitors and other early charitable organizations were sometimes limited in whom they would serve, often providing help and information only to those with their same moral views and religious backgrounds.

People with severe disabilities were often confined to mental-health institutions. By the late 18th century, many states and counties had built these facilities, then referred to as insane asylums, for the 24-hour care of people suffering from mental retardation to paralysis. The patients of these hospitals were often committed against their will by relatives. Few efforts were made to help patients return to society to lead normal, active lives.

The settlement houses of the late 19th century, such as Jane Addams's Hull House of Chicago, led to the development of more sensitive and enlightened ways to help people. Social workers lived among the residents, listening and learning along with them. But even with this new understanding of social work, those with disabilities were still unable to get complete assistance. Society wanted to help those in need but didn't necessarily want to live among them. As a result, separate schools, workplaces, and agencies for the disabled were established. Although social workers instructed blind people in how to cook and clean, how to use a guide dog, and how to read Braille, they made few efforts to integrate them into the community.

Legal efforts to end this discrimination began with the 1920 Vocational Rehabilitation Act. This act led to the development of state and federal agencies focused on enhancing the employment opportunities for people with disabilities. Over the years, this act has broadened to include job counseling and retraining services and the provision of prosthetic and other assisting devices. Recent efforts toward ending discrimination in employment and public services include the 1990 Americans with Disabilities Act.

The Job

Although he was diagnosed with multiple sclerosis years ago, Ken Smith has only recently required the use of a wheelchair. He also has only partial use of his right hand. For the last few years, he has worked as a newspaper journalist, driving himself to crime scenes, taking notes during interviews, and writing at a frantic pace to keep up with the pace of the newsroom. Now that he requires a wheelchair to get around, he is going to have to make many adjustments in his life. Fortunately for Smith, there are a number of services and benefits to help him—he just needs to know how to find this help.

The simple act of providing information is one of the most important jobs of an orientation and mobility specialist. These workers help to direct people like Smith to the many agencies available that assist those with vision and mobility impairments. By listening carefully to the problem, orientation and mobility specialists determine the best route for assistance, contact the agency on behalf of the client, and make sure they receive the proper assistance. Because of limited funding and support, disability services are often unable to promote themselves. The biggest problem facing communities is not the lack of services available, but the lack of public awareness of these outlets.

However, Smith will require much more than names and phone numbers from an orientation and mobility specialist. Smith not only needs to find the right wheelchair, but also needs instruction on how to use it. His home needs to be analyzed to determine what modifications need to be made (e.g., wheelchair ramps, handrails, wider doorways). If the necessary modifications cannot be made, he will have to consider moving to a new place. For all of these somewhat daunting decisions, Smith can ask an orientation and mobility specialist for advice.

Smith's workplace may also require modifications. Though perfectly capable of continuing his work as a journalist, Smith is going to have to fulfill his duties in different ways. For example, a special car may be required. Because of the limited use of his hand, he may need a modified computer keyboard or an assistant. An orientation and mobility specialist can serve as a client's advocate, negotiating with employers to prevent any cause for discrimination in the workplace. Specialists may also offer training and education programs to integrate or reintegrate the client into the workplace.

An orientation and mobility specialist also serves as a counselor. A client may need individual therapy or a support group. The family of the client may also need counseling on how to adjust to a parent or child's disability.

In addition to offering services that directly benefit the client (counseling, advocacy, education, and referral), some specialists may offer services that have indirect benefits for clients. These additional services include outreach, publicity, planning, and research. Because of a general lack of awareness of the social services available, orientation and mobility specialists may focus on ways to educate the public about the challenges facing those with disabilities. They may lead fund-raising efforts for research or programs aimed at assisting the disabled community.

Requirements

High School

To improve your communication skills, take high school courses such as English, composition, speech, and journalism. Courses in history, social studies, and sociology are also recommended.

Because a large part of the job is providing information about disability services, you should be comfortable using the Internet and various computer programs. Not only will you have to be able to work with computers yourself, you may be required to teach clients how to use these resources, too.

To gain familiarity with information services, check out employment opportunities to work as an administrative assistant or aide at your local library.

Postsecondary Training

The Association for Education and Rehabilitation of the Blind and Visually Impaired provides a listing of approved orientation and mobility programs at the graduate, undergraduate, and certification-only levels. Programs include instruction in mobility techniques, where students simulate blindness or limited vision with blindfolds or other devices. Internships with disability agencies are also incorporated into the programs.

Other specialists prepare themselves for the career by studying social work. The Council on Social Work Education requires that five areas be covered in accredited bachelor's degree social work programs: human behavior and the social environment, social welfare policy and services, social work practice, research, and field practicum. Most programs require two years of liberal arts study, followed by two years of study in the social work major. Also, students must complete a field practicum of at least 400 clock hours.

Though some starting positions require only a bachelor's degree, most supervisory and administrative positions within social work require further education. Graduate programs are organized according to fields of practice (e.g., mental health care), problem areas (e.g., substance abuse), population groups (e.g., the elderly), and practice roles (e.g., practice with individuals, families or communities). They are usually two-year programs, with at least 900 hours of field practice. Doctoral degrees are also available for those interested in research, planning, or community outreach jobs.

Certification or Licensing

Only selected states require orientation and mobility specialists to be certified. The Academy for Certification of Vision Rehabilitation and Education Professionals offers certification to those who meet certain educational and experience requirements. To be eligible to sit the certification exam, individuals must first complete an approved orientation and mobility program.

Other Requirements

For years, people with disabilities have faced discrimination. This discrimination is fueled by fear, misunderstanding, and by the way people with disabilities are represented in popular culture. Orientation and mobility specialists must be able to honestly address their own perceptions of people with disabilities. Specialists must be sensitive to the client's situation and have a genuine interest in involving that person in the community and workplace.

Specialists also work frequently with the elderly, requiring understanding of the aging experience. Workers must be patient and be good listeners to provide the elderly with the supportive network they need.

Communication skills are also very important. Much of the work as an orientation and mobility specialist involves talking and listening to clients, teaching, interviewing, and counseling. You will need to provide clear instructions to the client, their family, and their employer.

Because many of the problems facing those with disabilities stem from discrimination, many specialists work to educate the public about living with disabilities through research, reports, and fund-raising.

Exploring

Aspiring specialists can explore Web sites concerning disabilities and social work. A job in the school or public library helping people conduct research will put your information retrieval skills to good use. Working on the school newspaper will also help you develop your writing, researching and interviewing skills—all important aspects of social work.

Part-time data entry jobs at a hospital or long-term care facility can familiarize you with medical terminology and the services available to people with disabilities. A part-time job in a retail pharmacy will involve you directly with people with disabilities and also the services that pay for the rental and purchase of wheelchairs, walkers, and canes. You can also gain experience by volunteering at any social service agency to get a sense of the work environment and responsibilities.

Employers

Orientation and mobility specialists can find work with for-profit, nonprofit, and public programs. They may work in hospitals and community agencies such as transitional living services, or with private agencies that focus on providing services specifically to those with disabilities.

An orientation and mobility specialist may also be self-employed, providing service on a contract basis to individuals or social service agencies.

Starting Out

To gain experience in social work, consider working with a social service agency specializing in information and referral. Rehabilitation centers, senior homes, schools, and summer camps for the blind, visually impaired, and disabled also offer many opportunities for experience. Because of limited funding, staffing may consist of only a few social work professionals, and the rest may be volunteers or assistants. Volunteer work may lead to full-time employment or simply introduce you to other social work professionals who can provide career guidance and letters of reference.

Advancement

Orientation and mobility specialists may advance to become supervisors of assistants or executive directors of rehabilitation agencies. Another possible route for advancement is through teaching.

The more challenging and better-paying jobs tend to go to those with more years of practical experience and higher degrees. Further study, extensive experience, and good references will lead to advancement in the profession. Also, many social work programs offer continuing education workshops, courses, and seminars. These refresher courses help practicing specialists refine their skills and learn about new areas of practice, methods, and problems. These courses are intended to supplement previous education, not substitute for a bachelor's or master's degree. Continuing education can lead to job promotions and salary increases.

Earnings

The higher the degree held by specialists, the higher their earning potential. Those with a Ph.D. can take jobs in indirect service, research, and planning. Salaries also vary among regions; in general, social workers on the east and west coasts earn higher salaries than those in the Midwest. During the first five years of practice, salaries increase faster than in later years.

General social workers earned a median annual salary of $30,590 in 1998, according to the *Occupational Outlook Handbook*. The lowest 10 percent earned less than $19,250 and the top 10 percent earned over $49,080.

Specialists who work in school systems are generally paid on the same scale as other teachers in the system. Those who work for private clients are usually paid by the hour or per session.

Work Environment

Orientation and mobility specialists work part of the time in an office, analyzing and updating client files, interviewing clients over the phone, and talking with other service agencies. Depending on the size of the agency, office duties such as typing letters, filing, and answering phones may be performed by an aide or volunteer.

The rest of their time is spent outside the office, interacting directly with clients and others. Orientation and mobility specialists are involved directly with the people they serve and must carefully examine their clients' living conditions and family relations.

Advocacy involves work in a variety of different environments; it involves meetings with clients' employers, agency directors, and local legislators. Should the client press charges for discrimination, orientation and mobility specialists may be called upon to testify in court.

Both counseling and advocacy can be stressful aspects of the work, but helping to empower people with disabilities can be very rewarding.

Outlook

Because disabilities are so loosely defined, it is difficult to determine exactly how many people live with them. According to WebMD, experts estimate the U.S. disabled population to be approximately 43 million people—a large segment of society. In addition to continuing the fight against discrimination, the disabled will also need assistance to live productive lives.

Future funding is an important consideration for social service agencies. In many cases, the agencies providing information and referral must compete for funding with the very programs to which they refer people. This calls for good relationships between agencies and services. In order for agencies to receive adequate funding, social workers, including orientation and mobility specialists, must conduct research and provide reports to federal, state, and local governments showing proof of financial need. Their reports help to illustrate where funds should be allocated to best serve the disabled community.

The employment of orientation and mobility specialists is expected to grow at a faster-than-average rate. Specialists will continue to increase public awareness of the importance of aid for the disabled and visually impaired. Assistance services will continue to make their way into more public areas, such as libraries, workplaces, and other public facilities.

New computer technology has and will continue to cater to the special needs of the disabled. The development of specialized equipment and the expansion of the World Wide Web allows the disabled and visually impaired to access online resources for assistance. Orientation and mobility specialists will be needed to help those with disabilities use new technology to their best advantage.

For More Information

For information on certification, contact:

**Academy for Certification of Vision Rehabilitation
and Education Professionals**
PO Box 91047
Tucson, AZ 85752-10047
Tel: 520-887-6816
Email: info@acvrep.org
Web: http://www.acvrep.org/

For information on educational programs, contact the following organizations:

**Association for Education and Rehabilitation
of the Blind and Visually Impaired**
4600 Duke Street, #430
PO Box 22397
Alexandria, VA 22304
Tel: 703-823-9690
Web: http://www.aerbvi.org/

Council on Social Work Education
1725 Duke Street, Suite 500
Alexandria, VA 22314-3457
Tel: 703-683-8080
Email: info@cswe.org
Web: http://www.cswe.org

For information about careers, education, and job leads, contact:

National Association of Social Workers
750 First Street, NE, Suite 700
Washington, DC 20002-4241
Tel: 800-638-8799
Web: http://www.socialworkers.org

For career information and job listings available in Canada, contact:

Canadian Association of Social Workers
383 Parkdale Avenue, Suite 402
Ottawa, ON K1Y 4R4 Canada
Tel: 613-729-6668
Email: casw@casw-acts.ca
Web: http://www.casw-acts.ca/

Psychiatric Technicians

Health Psychology	School Subjects
Communication/ideas Helping/teaching	Personal Skills
Primarily indoors Primarily one location	Work Environment
Some postsecondary training	Minimum Education Level
$10,000 to $25,000 to $40,000	Salary Range
Required by certain states	Certification or Licensing
About as fast as the average	Outlook

Overview

Psychiatric technicians work with mentally ill, emotionally disturbed, or developmentally disabled people. Their duties vary considerably depending on place of work but may include helping patients with hygiene and housekeeping and recording patients' pulse, temperature, and respiration rate. Psychiatric technicians participate in treatment programs by having one-on-one sessions with patients, under the direction of a nurse or counselor.

Another prime aspect of the psychiatric technician's work is reporting observations of patients' behavior to medical and psychiatric staff. Psychiatric technicians may also fill out admitting forms for new patients, contact patients' families to arrange conferences, issue medications from the dispensary, and maintain records. There are approximately 66,000 psychiatric technicians employed in the United States.

History

Although some mentally ill people were treated as early as the 15th century in institutions like the Hospital of Saint Mary of Bethlehem in London (whose name was often shortened to Bedlam, hence the modern word "bedlam"), the practice of institutionalizing people with mental disorders did not become common until the 17th century.

During the 17th, 18th, and even into the 19th centuries, treatment of mentally ill patients was quite crude and often simply barbarous. This state of affairs started to change as medical practitioners began to see mental illness as a medical problem. During the late 18th and early 19th centuries, hospitals began concentrating on keeping patients clean and comfortable, building their self-respect, and treating them with friendliness and encouragement. This conception of mental illness treatment resulted in the establishment of specially designed institutions for the care of mental patients.

Beginning in the 1940s, mental health institutions sought more effective therapeutic services for their patients, including more social activities and innovative treatment programs. Treatment shifted from a sole reliance on state mental hospitals to provision of more services in general hospitals and community mental health centers.

The object was to shorten periods of institutionalization and to decrease the stigma and dislocation associated with treatment in mental hospitals. However, these changes also sharply increased personnel needs. One strategy for dealing with this has been to train more professionals—psychiatrists, psychologists, social workers, nurses, and others. Another strategy has focused on training more nonprofessionals—aides, attendants, orderlies, and others.

The drive to develop new therapies and the trend toward deinstitutionalizing patients have led to the creation of a new category of mental health worker with a training level between that of the professional and the nonprofessional. Workers at this level are usually referred to as paraprofessionals or technicians, and in the mental health field they are known as psychiatric technicians or mental health technicians.

The Job

Psychiatric technicians not only take over for or assist professionals in traditional treatment activities but also provide new services in innovative ways.

They may work with alcohol and drug abusers, psychotic or emotionally disturbed children and adults, developmentally disabled people, or the aged. They must be skilled and specially trained.

Psychiatric technicians are supervised by health professionals, such as registered nurses, counselors, therapists, or, more and more frequently, senior psychiatric technicians. Psychiatric technicians work as part of a team of mental health care workers and provide physical and mental rehabilitation for patients through recreational, occupational, and psychological readjustment programs.

In general, psychiatric technicians help plan and implement individual treatment programs. Specific activities vary according to work setting, but they may include the following: interviewing and information gathering; working in a hospital unit admitting, screening, evaluating, or discharging patients; record keeping; making referrals to community agencies; working for patients' needs and rights; visiting patients at home after their release from a hospital; and participating in individual and group counseling and therapy.

Psychiatric technicians endeavor to work with patients in a broad, comprehensive manner and to see each patient as a person whose peculiar or abnormal behavior stems from an illness or disability. They strive to help each patient achieve a maximum level of functioning. This means helping patients strengthen social and mental skills, accept greater responsibility, and develop confidence to enter into social, educational, or vocational activities.

In addition, psychiatric technicians working in hospitals handle a certain number of nursing responsibilities. They may take temperatures, pulses and respiration rates; measure blood pressures; and help administer medications and physical treatments. In many cases, technicians working in hospitals will find themselves concerned with all aspects of their patients' lives—from eating, sleeping, and personal hygiene to developing social skills and improving self-image.

Technicians working in clinics, community mental health centers, halfway houses, day hospitals, or other noninstitutional settings also perform some activities special to their situation. They interview newly registered patients and their relatives and visit patients and their families at home. They also administer psychological tests, participate in group activities, and write reports about their observations to supervising psychiatrists or other mental health professionals. They try to ease the transition of patients leaving hospitals and returning to their communities. They may refer patients to and arrange for consultations with mental health specialists. They may also help patients resolve problems with employment, housing, and personal finance.

Most psychiatric technicians are trained as generalists in providing mental health services. But some opportunities exist for technicians to specialize in a particular aspect of mental health care. For example, some psychiatric technicians specialize in the problems of mentally disturbed children. Others work as counselors in drug and alcohol abuse programs or as members of psychiatric emergency or crisis-intervention teams.

Another area of emphasis is working in community mental health. Technicians employed in this area are sometimes known as *human services technicians.* They use rehabilitation techniques for nonhospitalized patients who have problems adjusting to their social environment. These technicians may be primarily concerned with drug and alcohol abuse, parental effectiveness, the elderly, or problems in interpersonal relationships. Human services technicians work in social welfare departments, child care centers, preschools, vocational rehabilitation workshops, and schools for the learning disabled, emotionally disturbed, and mentally handicapped. This concentration is particularly popular in college curriculums, according to the American Association of Psychiatric Technicians, although it has yet to find wide acceptance in the job market.

With slightly different training, psychiatric technicians may specialize in the treatment of developmentally disabled people. These technicians, sometimes referred to as *DD techs,* work with patients by doing such things as teaching recreational activities. They generally work in halfway houses, state hospitals, training centers, or state and local service agencies. These jobs are among the easiest psychiatric technician jobs to get, and many techs start out in this area. On average, however, the pay of the DD tech is considerably less than that of other psychiatric technicians.

Requirements

High School

A high school diploma is the minimum education requirement to find work as a psychiatric technician, although in many cases psychiatric technicians are expected to have two years of training beyond high school. In general, high school students should take courses in English, biology, psychology, and sociology.

Postsecondary Training

The two-year postsecondary training programs usually lead to an associate of arts or associate of science degree. It is important to note that many hospitals prefer to hire applicants with bachelor's degrees.

In general, study programs include human development, personality structure, the nature of mental illness, and to a limited extent, anatomy, physiology, basic nursing, and medical science. Other subjects usually include some introduction to basic social sciences so that technicians can better understand relevant family and community structures; an overview of structure and functions of institutions that treat patients; and most important, practical instruction.

Certification and Licensing

Psychiatric technicians must be licensed in California, Colorado, Kansas, and Arkansas. Certification is voluntary in most other states. Prospective technicians and technicians-in-training should consult their guidance or placement counselors for more information about requirements in their states. Certification is available through the American Association of Psychiatric Technicians. Level 1 techs must have a high school diploma and pass a written test. Level 2 techs must have 30 semester credits and one year of experience and pass a written test. Level 3 techs must have an associate's degree and two years of experience and pass a written test. Level 4 techs must have a bachelor's degree and three years of experience and pass a written test.

Most mental health technology programs emphasize interviewing skills. Such training guides technicians to correctly describe a patient's tone of voice and body language so that they are well equipped to observe and record behavior that will be interpreted by the treatment team, and sometimes even a court of law. Some programs also teach administration of selected psychological tests. You may also gain knowledge and training in crisis intervention techniques, child guidance, group counseling, family therapy, behavior modification, and consultation skills.

Other Requirements

Because psychiatric technicians interact with people, you must be sensitive to others' needs and feelings. Some aspects of sensitivity can be learned, but this requires a willingness to listen, being extremely observant, and risking involvement in situations that at first may seem ambiguous and confusing. In addition, you need to be willing to look at your own attitudes and behavior and to be flexible and open about effecting changes in them. The more you know of yourself, the more effective you will be in helping others.

Patience, understanding, and a "thick skin" are required in working with people who may be disagreeable and unpleasant because of their illnesses. Patients can be particularly adept at finding a person's weaknesses and exploiting them. This is not a job for the tenderhearted. A sense of responsibility and the ability to remain calm in emergencies are also essential characteristics.

Exploring

Prospective psychiatric technicians can gather personal experience in this field in a number of ways. You can apply for a job as a nurse's aide at a local general hospital. In this way you gain direct experience providing patient care. If such a job requires too much of a time commitment, you might consider volunteering at a hospital part-time or during the summer. Volunteering is an excellent way to become acquainted with the field, and many techs' full-time jobs evolve from volunteer positions. Most volunteers must be 21 years of age to work in the mental health unit. Younger students who are interested in volunteering can often find places in the medical records department or other areas to get their feet in the door.

People interested in this career might also consider volunteering at their local mental health association or a local social welfare agency. In some cases, the mental health association can arrange opportunities for volunteer work inside a mental hospital or mental health clinic. Finally, either on your own or with your teachers, you can arrange a visit to a mental health clinic. You may be able to talk with staff members and observe first-hand how psychiatric technicians do their jobs.

Employers

Psychiatric technicians work in a variety of settings: the military, hospitals, mental hospitals, community mental health centers, psychiatric clinics, schools and day centers for the developmentally disabled, and social service agencies. They also work at residential and nonresidential centers, such as geriatric nursing homes, child or adolescent development centers, and halfway houses.

Other potential places of employment for psychiatric technicians include correctional programs and juvenile courts, schools for the blind and deaf, community action programs, family service centers, and public housing programs.

Starting Out

Graduates from mental health and human services technology programs can usually choose from a variety of job possibilities. College placement officers can be extremely helpful in locating employment. Students can follow want ads or apply directly to clinics, agencies, or hospitals of their choice. Job information can also be obtained from the department of mental health in each state.

Advancement

Working as a psychiatric technician is still a relatively new occupation, and sequences of promotions have not yet been clearly defined. Seeking national certification through the American Association of Psychiatric Technicians is one way to help to set up a career path in this field. Advancement normally takes the form of being given greater responsibilities with less supervision. It usually results from gaining experience, developing competence and leadership abilities, and continuing formal and practical education. In cases where promotions are governed by civil service regulations, advancement is based on experience and test scores on promotion examinations.

In large part, advancement is linked to gaining further education. Thus, after working a few years, technicians may decide to obtain a bachelor's degree in psychology. Advanced education, coupled with previous training and work experience, greatly enhance advancement potential. For instance, with a bachelor's degree, experienced technicians may be able to find rewarding positions as instructors in programs to train future mental health workers.

Earnings

Salaries for psychiatric technicians vary according to geographical area and work setting: technicians in California generally receive substantially higher wages than those in other areas of the country, and technicians in community settings generally receive higher salaries than those in institutional settings. On average, psychiatric technicians receive starting salaries ranging anywhere from minimum wage, or less than $10,000 a year, to as much as $20,000 a year or more. Most technicians are hourly employees, receiving $7 to $12 an hour, some even as high as $15 an hour. With increased experience, technicians can expect at least modest increases in their salaries each year. Some senior psychiatric technicians earn as much as $27,000 a year or more (those in California can earn as much as $35,000 to $40,000 a year or more with 10 to 15 years of experience).

Most psychiatric technicians receive fringe benefits, including hospitalization insurance, sick leave, and paid vacations. Technicians working for state institutions or agencies will probably also be eligible for financial assistance for further education.

Work Environment

Psychiatric technicians work in a variety of settings and their working conditions vary accordingly. Typically they work 40 hours a week, five days a week, although one may be a weekend day. Some psychiatric technicians work evening or night shifts, and all technicians may sometimes be asked to work holidays.

For the most part, the physical surroundings are pleasant. Most institutions, clinics, mental health centers, and agency offices are kept clean and comfortably furnished. Technicians who work with the mentally ill must nonetheless adjust to an environment that is normally chaotic and sometimes upsetting. Some patients are acutely depressed and withdrawn or excessively agitated and excited. Some patients may become unexpectedly violent and verbally abusive. However, institutions treating these kinds of patients maintain enough staff to keep the patients safe and to protect workers from physical harm. Psychiatric technicians who make home visits also may sometimes confront unpleasant conditions.

Finally, psychiatric technicians work not only with individuals but often with the community. In that role, technicians can be called upon to advocate for their patients by motivating community agencies to provide services or obtaining exceptions to rules when needed for individuals or groups of patients. Successful psychiatric technicians become competent in working and dealing with various decision-making processes of community and neighborhood groups.

Outlook

The number of psychiatric technicians in the United States is estimated at about 66,000. This number is expected to rise because of, in large part, a well-established trend of returning hospitalized patients to their communities after shorter and shorter periods of hospitalization. The trend has encouraged development of comprehensive community mental health centers and has led to an increased need for psychiatric technicians to staff these facilities.

Concerns over rising health care costs should increase employment levels for technicians, because they and other paraprofessionals can take over some functions of higher-paid professionals. This kind of substitution has been demonstrated to be an effective way of reducing costs without reducing quality of care.

For More Information

For information on becoming a nationally certified psychiatric technician, contact:

American Association of Psychiatric Technicians
PO Box 928
Orem, UT 85059-0928
Tel: 800-391-7589
Web: http://psych-health.com/aapt.htm

For more information on the career, check out the following Web site:

California Association of Psychiatric Technicians
Web: http://www.psych-health.com

Psychiatrists

	School Subjects
Biology Psychology Sociology	

	Personal Skills
Helping/teaching Technical/scientific	

	Work Environment
Primarily indoors Primarily one location	

	Minimum Education Level
Medical degree	

	Salary Range
$121,000 to $150,610 to $207,498	

	Certification or Licensing
Required by all states	

	Outlook
Faster than the average	

Overview

Psychiatrists are physicians who attend to patients' mental, emotional, and behavioral symptoms. They try to help people function better in their daily lives. Different kinds of psychiatrists use different treatment methods depending on their fields. They may explore a patient's beliefs and history. They may prescribe medicine, including tranquilizers, antipsychotics, and antidepressants. If they specialize in treating children, they may use play therapy.

History

The greatest advances in psychiatric treatment came in the latter part of the 19th century. Emil Kraepelin, a German psychiatrist, made an important contribution when he developed a classification system for mental illnesses that is still used for diagnosis. Sigmund Freud (1856-1939), the famous

Viennese psychiatrist, developed techniques for analyzing human behavior that have strongly influenced the practice of modern psychiatry. Freud first lectured in the United States in 1909. Swiss psychiatrist Carl Jung (1875-1961), a former associate of Freud's, revolutionized the field with his theory of a collective unconscious.

Another great change in treatment began in the 1950s with the development of medication that could be used in treating psychiatric problems, such as depression and anxiety.

The Job

Psychiatrists are medical doctors (M.D.s) who treat people suffering from mental and emotional illnesses that make it hard for them to cope with everyday living or to behave in socially acceptable ways. Problems treated range from being irritable and feeling frustrated to losing touch with reality. Some people, in addition to having a mental illness, may also engage in destructive behavior such as abusing alcohol or drugs or committing crimes. Others may have physical symptoms that spring from mental or emotional disorders. People with mental illness were once so misunderstood and stigmatized by society that they were kept, chained and shackled, in asylums. Today society recognizes that emotional or mental illnesses need to be diagnosed and treated just like any other medical problem.

Some psychiatrists run general practices, treating patients with a variety of mental disorders. Others may specialize in working with certain types of therapy or kinds of patients, for example, the chronically ill. When meeting a client for the first time, psychiatrists conduct an evaluation of the client. This involves talking with the person about his or her current circumstances and getting a medical history. In some cases, the psychiatrist will give the client a physical examination or order laboratory tests if he or she feels the client's problem may have a physical cause. Next, the psychiatrist decides on a treatment plan for the client. This may involve medications, psychotherapy, or a combination of these.

As medical doctors, psychiatrists can prescribe medication that affects a client's mood or behavior, such as tranquilizers or antidepressants. Scientific advancements in both the understanding of how the human brain functions and the creation of more effective drugs with fewer side effects have helped make medications an important element in the treatment of mental illness. Some psychiatrists will only supervise the medication aspect of a client's treatment and refer the client to another health professional, such as a psychologist, for the psychotherapy aspect of treatment. These psychiatrists, who may typically work in private practice in large cities, focus on the chemical aspects of a person's illness and find medication to help that client. Other psychiatrists, often those working in hospitals or in small cities and towns, may be the providers of both medication management and pscyhotherapy.

Psychotherapy, sometimes called talk therapy, is perhaps the most well-known type of treatment for mental illness—even cartoons have depicted a patient lying on a couch and telling his problems to a doctor who is writing copious notes. Although pop culture may exaggerate these elements for humor, the depiction of talk therapy as talking is basically correct. By having the client talk about problems he or she faces, the therapist helps the client uncover and understand the feelings and ideas that form the root of the client's problems and, thus, overcome emotional pain. Talk therapy can be used with individuals, groups, couples, or families.

Another therapy method used by some psychiatrists is behavior therapy or behavior modification therapy. This therapy focuses on changing a client's behavior and may involve teaching the client to use meditation and relaxation techniques as well as other treatment methods, such as biofeedback, a process in which a person uses electronic monitors to measure the effects that thoughts and feelings have on bodily functions like muscle tension, heart rate, or brain waves. This is done so that the client can learn how to consciously control his or her body through stress reduction.

Free association is a technique in which the client is encouraged to relax and talk freely. The therapist's aim is to help the client uncover troubling subconscious beliefs or conflicts and their causes. Dreams may also be examined for hints about the unconscious mind. Subconscious conflicts are believed to cause neurosis, which is an emotional disorder in which the patient commonly exhibits anxious behavior.

In addition to seeing clients, psychiatrists may also work with other health care professionals in the course of treating clients. Dr. Jenny Kane, who is in charge of a psychiatric ward of a hospital, for example, notes that meetings are an important part of her work. "At least three to four times a week, we have treatment planning meetings. These meetings are multidisciplinary, so anyone who is involved with treating the patient is in attendance."

In addition to those working in general psychiatry, there are psychiatrists who specialize in working with certain groups or in certain areas. These specialists include:

Child psychiatrists work with youth and usually their parents as well.

At the opposite end of the age scale are *geriatric psychiatrists,* who specialize in working with older individuals.

Industrial psychiatrists are employed by companies to deal with problems that affect employee performance, such as alcoholism or absenteeism.

Forensic psychiatrists work in the field of law. They evaluate defendants and testify on their mental state. They may help determine whether or not defendants understand the charges against them and if they can contribute to their own defense.

No matter what their specialty, however, psychiatrists must deal compassionately with clients. Dr. Kane says, "You must be able to empathize with them, you must have a desire to help them. If that is lacking, I would imagine that you'd be constantly frustrated in your patient dealings." In her position at the hospital, Kane sometimes sees people who come in with frostbite, infections, or other medical complications because they haven't been able to care for themselves physically. In these circumstances, a psychiatrist's medical training in dealing with the body comes into play. "I treat anything that a family practitioner would treat," Kane explains. "If it's necessary, I call in a specialist."

Other health professionals who may work with mentally ill people include psychologists, who may see clients but are unable to prescribe medications because they are not physicians, and *neurologists*, physicians specializing in problems of the nervous system. In some cases, a person's disturbed behavior results from disorders of the nervous system, and neurologists diagnose and treat these conditions.

Requirements

High School

If working as a psychiatrist sounds interesting to you, you should start preparing yourself for college and medical school while you are still in high school. Do this by taking a college preparatory curriculum and concentrating on math and science classes. Biology, chemistry, and physics as well as algebra, geometry, and calculus will all be helpful. You can also start learning about human behavior by taking psychology, sociology, and history classes. In addition, take English classes to develop your communication skills— much of this work involves speaking, listening, and record keeping.

Postsecondary Training

When you are deciding what college to attend, keep in mind that you'll want one with a strong science department, excellent laboratory facilities, and a strong humanities department. You may want to check out the publication *Medical School Admissions Requirements* by the Association of American Medical Colleges (AAMC) to see what specific college classes you should take in preparation for medical school. Some colleges or universities offer a "premed" major, other possible majors include chemistry and biology. No matter what your major, though, you can count on taking biology, chemistry, organic chemistry, physics, and psychology classes. Medical schools look for well-rounded individuals, however, so be sure to take other classes in the humanities and social sciences. The AAMC reports that most people apply to medical school after their junior year of college. Most medical schools require the Medical College Admission Test as part of their application, so you should take this test your junior or even sophomore year.

In medical school, students must complete a four-year program of medical studies and supervised clinical work leading to their M.D. degrees. The first two years you will once again concentrate on studying the sciences; in addition, you will learn about taking a person's medical history and how to do an examination. The next two years are devoted to clinical work, which is when you first begin to see patients under supervision.

After receiving an M.D., physicians who plan to specialize in psychiatry must complete a residency. In the first year, they work in several specialties, such as internal medicine and pediatrics. Then they work for three years in a psychiatric hospital or a general hospital's psychiatric ward. Here they learn how to diagnose and treat various mental and emotional disorders or illnesses. Some psychiatrists continue their education beyond this four-year residency. To become a child psychiatrist, for example, a doctor must train for at least three years in general residency and two years in child psychiatry residency. Part of psychiatrists' training involves undergoing therapy themselves.

Certification or Licensing

All physicians must be licensed in order to practice medicine. After completing the M.D., graduates must pass the licensing test given by the board of medical examiners for the state in which they want to work. Following their residency, psychiatrists must take and pass a certifying exam given by the Board of Psychiatry and Neurology. They then receive the designation Diplomates in Psychiatry.

Other Requirements

To complete the required studies and training, students need outstanding mental ability and perseverance. Psychiatrists must be emotionally stable so they can deal with their patients objectively. "Working with emotional disturbances on a daily basis can be draining and exhausting—even discouraging," notes Dr. Jenny Kane. "Of course, the flip side is when you see people improve, when you know without a doubt that you've helped them. That's a real high." Psychiatrists must be perceptive, able to listen well, and able to work well with others. They must also be dedicated to a lifetime of learning, as new therapeutic techniques and medications are constantly being developed.

Exploring

You can easily explore this job by reading as much as you can about the field and the work. To find out what professionals consider worthwhile resources, you may want to read the *Authoritative Guide to Self-Help Resources in Mental Health,* by John Norcross and others (Guilford Publications, New York: 2000). To learn about different types of psychotherapies, you may want to read *Essential Psychotherapies: Theory and Practice,* edited by Alan Gurman and Stanley Messer (Guilford Publications, New York: 1997). Talk with your guidance counselor or psychology teacher about helping you arrange an informational interview with a local psychiatrist. If this is not possible, try to get an informational interview with any physician, such as your family doctor, to ask about the medical school experience.

An excellent way to explore this type of work is to do volunteer work in health care settings, such as hospitals, clinics, or nursing homes. While you may not be taking care of people with psychiatric problems, you will be interacting with patients and health care professionals. This experience will benefit you when it's time to apply to medical schools as well as give you a feel for working with the ill.

Employers

Approximately half of practicing psychiatrists work in private practice; many others combine private practice with work in a health care institution. These institutions include private hospitals, state mental hospitals, medical schools, community health centers, and government health agencies. Psychiatrists may also work at correctional facilities, for health maintenance organizations, or in nursing homes. They are employed throughout the country.

Starting Out

Psychiatrists in residency can find job leads in professional journals and through professional organizations such as the American Psychiatric Association. Many are offered permanent positions with the same institution where they complete their residency.

Advancement

Most psychiatrists advance in their careers by enlarging their knowledge and skills, clientele, and earnings. Those who work in hospitals, clinics, and mental health centers may become administrators. Those who teach or concentrate on research may become department heads.

Earnings

Psychiatrists' earnings are determined by the kind of practice they have and its location, their experience, and the number of patients they treat. Like other physicians, their average income is among the highest of any occupation.

In 1997, the median income for psychiatrists after expenses was $130,000 a year, according to the American Medical Association. A 2000 salary survey conducted by the placement firm Physicians Search found that physicians specializing in psychiatry and with three or more years of experience earned an average yearly income of $150,610. Reported salaries ranged from $121,000 to approximately $189,500 annually.

Psychiatrists on staff at psychiatric facilities earn an average salary of $126,585, according to a 1997 salary survey by The National Association of Psychiatric Health Systems. Psychiatric medical directors at such facilities earn an average of $150,890 a year, according to the survey. Psychiatrists who serve solely as chief executive officers of psychiatric facilities and who are not medical directors earn an average of $197,834 a year. Those who are CEOs and also medical directors make the highest average salaries, $207,498 a year.

Work Environment

Psychiatrists in private practice set their own schedules and usually work regular hours. They may work some evenings or weekends to see patients who cannot take time off during business hours. Most psychiatrists, however, put in long workdays, averaging 52 hours a week, according to American Medical Association statistics. Like other physicians, psychiatrists are always on call. Dr. Jenny Kane likens the obligations of her job to parenting. "Whatever and whenever a patient needs me, it's my job to be there—or at least to make arrangements to have them taken care of," she says.

Psychiatrists in private practice typically work in comfortable office settings. Some private psychiatrists also work as hospital staff members, consultants, lecturers, or teachers.

Salaried psychiatrists work in private hospitals, state hospitals, and community mental health centers. They also work for government agencies, such as the U.S. Department of Health and Human Services, the Department of Defense, and the Department of Veterans Affairs. Psychiatrists who work in public facilities often bear heavy workloads. Changes in treatment have reduced the number of patients in hospitals and have increased the number of patients in community health centers.

Outlook

The U.S. Department of Labor predicts employment for all physicians to grow faster than the average through 2008. Opportunities for psychiatrists in private practice and salaried positions are excellent. Demand is great for child psychiatrists, and other specialties are also in short supply, especially in rural areas and public facilities.

A number of factors contribute to this shortage. Growing population and increasing life span add up to more people who need psychiatric care; rising incomes enable more people to afford treatment; and higher educational levels make more people aware of the importance of mental health care. Medical insurance, although it usually limits the amount of mental health care, may provide some coverage. However, the amount of benefits being paid out has been more than cut in half over the past 10 years.

Psychiatrists are also needed as researchers to explore the causes of mental illness and develop new ways to treat it.

For More Information

For more information on becoming a doctor as well as current health care news, visit the AMA Web site:

American Medical Association (AMA)
515 North State Street
Chicago, IL 60610
Tel: 312-464-5000
Web: http://www.ama-assn.org

To read informative press releases about mental illness and health issues, check out the following Web site:

American Psychiatric Association
1400 K Street, NW
Washington, DC 20005
Tel: 888-357-7924
Email: apa@psych.org
Web: http://www.psych.org

To learn more about careers in medicine and how to apply to medical schools, visit the following Web site:

Association of American Medical College
2450 N Street, NW
Washington, DC 20037-1126
Tel: 202-828-0400
Web: http://www.aamc.org

For information on mental health issues, contact:

National Institute of Mental Health
Public Inquiries
6001 Executive Boulevard, Room 8184 MSC 9663
Bethesda, MD 20892
Tel: 301-443-4513
Email: nimhinfo@nih.gov
Web: http://www.nimh.nih.gov

To read the newsletter, **The Bell,** *which contains current information for the field, visit the NMHA's Web site:*

National Mental Health Association (NMHA)
1021 Prince Street
Alexandria, VA 22314-2971
Tel: 703-684-7722
Email: infoctr@nmha.org
Web: http://www.nmha.org

For information on education, advocacy, and certification for Canadian psychiatrists, contact:

Canadian Psychiatric Association
260-441 MacLaren Street
Ottawa, ON K2P-2H3 Canada
Tel: 613-234-2815
Email: cpa@cpa-apc.org
Web: http://www.cpa-apc.org

Psychologists

Biology Psychology Sociology	School Subjects
Helping/teaching Technical/scientific	Personal Skills
Primarily indoors Primarily one location	Work Environment
Master's degree	Minimum Education Level
$28,000 to $64,000 to $150,000+	Salary Range
Voluntary (certification) Required for certain positions (licensing)	Certification or Licensing
About as fast as the average	Outlook

Overview

Psychologists teach, counsel, conduct research, or administer programs to understand people and help people understand themselves. Psychologists examine individual and group behavior through testing, experimenting, and studying personal histories.

Psychologists normally hold doctorates in psychology. Unlike *psychiatrists*, they are not medical doctors and cannot prescribe medication.

History

The first syllable in psychology derives from "psyche," a Greek word meaning soul. The second half of psychology contains the root of the word "logic." Thus "psychology" translates as "the science of the soul."

Early philosophers emphasized differences between body and soul. Plato, for example, believed they were two entirely different parts. Modern scholars tend to emphasize the unity between mind and body rather than their dissimilarity.

The founder of experimental psychology, Wilhelm Wundt (1832-1920), held both an M.D. and a Ph.D. A physician, he taught at the University of Leipzig, where his title was Professor of Philosophy. Like Dr. Wundt, German scholars of the 19th century were committed to the scientific method. Discovery by experiment was considered the only respectable way for learned thinkers to work. Thus it was not thought strange that in 1879, Dr. Wundt set up an experimental laboratory to conduct research upon human behavior. Many people who later became famous U.S. psychologists received their training under Dr. Wundt.

At the turn of the 20th century, Russian physiologist Dr. Ivan Pavlov (1849-1936) discovered a key aspect of behaviorist theory while studying the process of digestion. While experimenting on dogs, he found that they began to salivate in anticipation of their food. He discovered that if he rang a bell before presenting their meat, the dogs associated the sound of a bell with mealtime. He then would ring the bell but withhold the food. The dogs' saliva flowed anyway, whether or not they saw or smelled food. Dr. Pavlov called this substitute stimulus a "conditioned response." Many psychologists began to incorporate the theory of conditioned response into theories of learning.

One of the most famous pioneers in psychology was Dr. Sigmund Freud (1856-1939), whose work led to many of the modern theories of behavior. Dr. Freud lived and practiced in Vienna, Austria, until Hitler's forces caused him to flee to England. His work on the meaning of dreams, the unconscious, and the nature of various emotional disturbances has had a profound effect upon the profession and practice of psychology for more than 60 years, although many psychologists now disagree with some of his theories.

Many Americans have contributed greatly to the science that seeks to understand human behavior: William James, Robert Woodworth, E. L. Thorndike, Clark Hull, B. F. Skinner, and others.

The Job

Psychology is both a science and a profession. As a science, it is a systematic approach to the understanding of people and their behavior; as a profession, it is the application of that understanding to help solve human problems. Psychology is a rapidly growing field, and psychologists work on a great variety of problems.

The field of psychology is so vast that no one person can become an expert in all phases of it. The psychologist usually concentrates on one specialty. Many of the specialties overlap in subject matter and methodology.

Many psychologists teach some area of basic psychology in colleges and universities. They are also likely to conduct research and supervise graduate student work in an area of special interest.

Clinical psychologists concern themselves with people's mental and emotional disorders. They assess and treat problems ranging from normal psychological crises, such as adolescent rebellion or middle-age loss of self-esteem, to extreme conditions, such as severe depression and schizophrenia.

Some clinical psychologists work almost exclusively with children. They may be staff members at a child guidance clinic or a treatment center for children at a large general hospital. *Child psychologists* and other clinical psychologists may engage in private practice, seeing clients at offices. Clinical psychologists comprise the largest group of specialists.

Developmental psychologists study development of people from birth through old age. They describe, measure, and explain age-related changes in behavior, stages of emotional development, universal traits and individual differences, and abnormal changes in development. Many developmental psychologists teach and do research in colleges and universities. Some specialize in programs for children in day care centers, preschools, hospitals, or clinics. Others specialize in programs for the elderly.

Social psychologists study how people interact with each other and how they are affected by their environment. Social psychology has developed from four sources: sociology, cultural anthropology, psychiatry, and psychology. Social psychologists are interested in individual and group behavior. They study the ways groups influence individuals and vice versa. They study different kinds of groups: ethnic, religious, political, educational, family, and many others. The social psychologist has devised ways to research group nature, attitudes, leadership patterns, and structure.

Counseling psychologists work with people who have problems they find difficult to face alone. These clients are not usually mentally or emotionally ill, but they are emotionally upset, anxious, or struggling with some conflict within themselves or their environment. By helping people solve their problems, make decisions, and cope with everyday stresses, the counseling psychologist actually is working in preventive mental health.

School psychologists frequently do diagnosis and remediation. They may engage primarily in preventive and developmental psychology. Many school psychologists are assigned the duty of testing pupils surmised to be exceptional. Other school psychologists work almost entirely with children who have proven to be a problem to themselves or to others and who have been referred for help by teachers or other members of the school system. Many school psychologists are concerned with pupils who reveal various kinds of learning disabilities. School psychologists may also be called upon to work with relationship problems between parents and children.

Industrial psychologists are concerned with the relation between people and work. They deal with organizational structure, worker productivity, job satisfaction, consumer behavior, personnel training and development, and the interaction between humans and machines. Industrial psychologists may work with a sales department to help salespeople become more effective. Some study assembly line procedures and suggest changes to reduce monotony and increase worker responsibility. Others plan various kinds of tests to help screen applicants for employment. Industrial psychologists conduct research to determine qualities that seem to produce the most efficient employees or help management develop programs to identify staff with management potential. They may be asked to investigate and report on certain differences of opinion between a supervisor and one of the workers. Some may design training courses to indoctrinate new employees or counsel older employees on career development or retirement preparation.

Other industrial psychologists, referred to as *engineering psychologists,* help engineers and technicians design systems that require workers or consumers and machines to interact. They also develop training aids for those systems.

Consumer psychologists are interested in consumer reactions to products or services. These psychologists may be asked to determine the kinds of products the public will buy. They may study, for instance, whether people prefer big cars or little cars. They might be asked to make decisions about the most appealing ways to present a product through advertising. Many of today's most established advertising, promotion, and packaging practices have been influenced by the opinions and advice of consumer psychologists. Consumer psychologists also try to improve product acceptability and safety in addition to helping the consumer make better decisions.

Psychometrists work with intelligence, personality, and aptitude tests used in clinics, counseling centers, schools, and businesses. They administer tests, score them, and interpret results as related to standard norms. Psychometrists also study methods and techniques used to acquire and evaluate psychological data. They may devise new, more reliable tests. These specialists are usually well trained in mathematics, statistics, and computer programming and technology.

The *educational psychologist* is concerned primarily with how people teach, learn, and evaluate learning. Many educational psychologists are employed on college or university faculties, and they also conduct research into learning theory. Some, however, are interested in evaluating learning.

Experimental psychologists conduct scientific experiments on particular aspects of behavior, either animal or human. Much experimental study is done in learning, in physiological psychology (the relationship of behavior to physiological processes), and in comparative psychology (sometimes called animal psychology). Many experimental psychological studies are carried out with animals, partly because their environments can be carefully controlled.

Many psychologists of all kinds find that writing skills are helpful. They may write up the results of research efforts for a scholarly journal. Some prepare papers for presentation at professional association meetings or sometimes write books or articles. Industrial psychologists may write instruction manuals. Educational psychologists may prepare test manuals.

Some psychologists become administrators who direct college or university psychology departments or personnel services programs in a school system or industry. Some become agency or department directors of research in scientific laboratories. They may be promoted to department head in a state or federal government agency. *Chief psychologists* in hospitals or psychiatric centers plan psychological treatment programs, direct professional and nonprofessional personnel, and oversee psychological services provided by the institution.

Requirements

High School

Because you will need to continue your education beyond high school in order to become a psychologist, you should enroll in college preparatory courses. Your class schedule should concentrate on English courses, computer science, mathematics, and sciences. Algebra, geometry, and calculus are important to take, as are biology, chemistry, and physics. Naturally you should take social science courses, such as psychology and sociology. You should also take a modern foreign language, such as French or German, because reading comprehension of these languages is one of the usual requirements for obtaining the doctorate degree.

Postsecondary Training

A doctorate in psychology (Ph.D. or Psy.D.) is recommended. While most new doctorates in the psychology field received a Ph.D., the number of Psy.D. recipients has more than doubled—to 16 percent—over the past decade. Some positions are available to people with a master's degree, but they are jobs of lesser responsibility and lower salaries than those open to people with a doctorate.

Psychology is an obvious choice for your college major, but not all graduate programs require entering students to have a psychology bachelor's degree. Nevertheless, your college studies should include a number of psychology courses, such as experimental psychology, developmental psychology, and abnormal psychology. You should also take classes in statistics as well as such classes as English, foreign language, and history to complete a strong liberal arts education.

Master's degree programs typically take two years to complete. Course work at this level usually involves statistics, ethics, and industrial and organizational content. If you want to work as a school psychologist, you will need to complete a supervised, year-long internship at a school after receiving your degree.

Some doctoral programs accept students with master's degrees; in other cases, students enter a doctoral program with only a bachelor's degree. Because these entrance requirements vary, you will need to research the programs you are interested in to find out their specific requirements. The doctorate degree typically takes between four and seven years to complete for those who begin their studies with only the bachelor's degree. Coursework will include studies in various areas of psychology and research (including work in quantitative research methods). Those who focus on research often complete a year-long postdoctoral fellowship. Those who want to work as clinical, counseling, or school psychologists must complete a one-year supervised internship. Frequently those who are interested in clinical, counseling, or school psychology will get the Psy.D. because this degree emphasizes clinical rather than research work. In addition, those interested in these three areas should attend a program accredited by the American Psychological Association.

Unlike psychiatrists, psychologists do not need to attend medical school.

Certification or Licensing

Psychologists in independent practice or those providing any type of patient care, such as clinical, counseling, and school psychologists, must be licensed or certified by the state in which they practice. Some states require the licensing of industrial/organizational psychologists. Because requirements vary, you will need to check with your state's licensing board for specific information.

The American Board of Professional Psychology offers voluntary specialty certification in a number of areas, including clinical psychology, group psychology, forensic psychology, rehabilitation psychology, and school psychology. Requirements for certification include having a doctorate in psychology, professional experience, appropriate postdoctoral training, and the passing of an examination. Those who fulfill these requirements receive the designation Diplomate.

Other Requirements

Because psychology is such a broad field, various personal attributes apply to different psychology positions. Those involved in research, for example, should be analytical, detail oriented, and have strong math and writing skills. Those working with patients should be "people persons," able to relate to others, and have excellent listening skills. No matter what their area of focus, however, all psychologists should be committed to lifelong learning since our understanding of humans is constantly evolving.

Exploring

If you are interested in psychology, explore the field by taking psychology classes in high school and reading all you can about the subject, including biographies of and works by noted psychologists. In addition, make an appointment to talk about the profession with a psychologist who may work at a nearby school, college, hospital, or clinic. Use the Internet to learn more about mental health issues by visiting Web sites, such as that of the National Mental Health Association at http://www.nmha.org or the American Psychological Association at http://www.apa.org.

If being involved with patient care interests you, gain experience in the health care field by volunteering at a local hospital or clinic. In addition, volunteer opportunities may exist at local nursing homes, where you will also have the chance to work with clients needing some type of assistance. If doing research work sounds appealing to you, consider joining your school's science club, which may offer the opportunity to work on projects, document the process, and work as part of a team.

Employers

Clinical psychologists may teach at colleges or universities. Or, clinical psychologists may work with patients in a private practice or a hospital, where they provide therapy after evaluation through special tests.

Many developmental psychologists teach and research in colleges and universities. Some specialize in programs for children in day care centers, preschools, hospitals, or clinics.

Social psychologists teach and conduct research in colleges or universities. They also work for agencies of the federal or state government or in private research firms. Some work as consultants. An increasing number of social psychologists work as researchers and personnel managers in such nontraditional settings as advertising agencies, corporations, and architectural and engineering firms.

Counseling psychologists work in college or university counseling centers; they also teach in psychology departments. They may be in private practice. Or they may work at a community health center, a marriage counseling agency, or a federal agency such as the Department of Veterans Affairs.

Consumer psychologists study consumer reactions to products or services. They are hired by advertising, promotion, and packaging companies.

Psychometrists may be employed in colleges and universities, testing companies, private research firms, or government agencies.

Educational psychologists may work for test publishing firms devising and standardizing tests of ability, aptitude, personal preferences, attitudes, or characteristics.

Starting Out

Those entering the field with only a bachelor's degree will face strong competition for few jobs. The university placement office or a psychology professor may be able to help such a student find a position assisting a psychologist at a health center or other location. Positions beyond the assistant level, however, will be very difficult to land. Those graduating from master's or doctorate degree programs will find more employment opportunities. Again, university placement offices may be able to provide these graduates with assistance. In addition, contacts made during an internship may offer job leads. Joining professional organizations and networking with members is also a way to find out about job openings. In addition, these organizations, such as the American Psychological Association, often list job vacancies in their publications for members.

Advancement

For those who have bachelor's or master's degrees, the first step to professional advancement is to complete a doctorate degree. After that, advancement will depend on the area of psychology in which the person is working. For example, a psychologist teaching at a college or university may advance through the academic ranks from instructor to professor. Some college teachers who enjoy administrative work become department heads.

Psychologists who work for state or federal government agencies may, after considerable experience, be promoted to head a section or department. School psychologists might become directors of pupil personnel services. Industrial psychologists can rise to managerial or administrative positions.

After several years of experience, many psychologists enter private practice or set up their own research or consulting firms.

Earnings

Because the psychology field offers so many different types of employment possibilities, salaries for psychologists vary greatly. In addition, the typical conditions affecting salaries, such as the person's level of education, professional experience, and location, also apply. A 1999 salary survey by the American Psychological Association reported member earnings for a number of positions, including the following.

The survey found assistant professors holding doctorate degrees and teaching in university psychology departments had a median salary for the nine to 10 month academic year of $41,000. Given these same conditions, associate professors had a median salary of $50,000, and full professors made a median of $72,000. Salaries for faculty will vary, however, depending on the type of institution at which they teach. For example, assistant professors with doctorate degrees teaching in a medical school's department of psychiatry earned a median salary for the nine to 10 month academic year of $49,000, according to the survey. Associate professors under these conditions reported a median income of $59,000, and full professors earned a median of $91,000.

For those holding a doctorate and working in education administrative positions, the survey found that those employed at universities and with 10 to 14 years of experience earned a median yearly salary of $62,500. Those with 20 to 24 years of experience made a median of $110,000 annually.

Psychologists with doctorates who choose to go into research will also find their earnings vary greatly based on employer. The salary survey, for example, found that those in research positions working in university psychology departments and having two to four years of experience made a median yearly salary of $28,000 in 1999. Those with the same education and experience level who worked for private research organizations, on the other hand, made a median yearly salary of $59,000.

Of the psychologists working directly with patients or clients, those with doctorates in clinical psychology and five to nine years of experience working in public general hospitals, VA hospitals, or individual private practice had median annual incomes ranging from approximately $60,000 to $64,000. Those in individual private practice with 15 to 19 years experience had a median income of $80,000, with those at the high end of the pay range earning more than $100,000.

Although they also work directly with clients, those with doctorates in school psychology reported somewhat lower earnings. For school psychologists working at elementary or secondary schools and with five to nine years of experience the median annual income was $57,000.

Psychologists with doctorate degrees in industrial/organizational psychology reported high incomes. Those with five to nine years of experience and working for consulting firms made a median yearly salary of $95,000, while those with the same amount of experience and working in business or industry earned a median of $87,000 annually. With 25 or more years in this field, some of these psychologists make more than $150,000.

Salaries for psychologists with master's degrees are generally much lower than those with doctorates. For example, those working as assistant professors in university psychology departments earned a median of $37,000 for the academic year in 1999, and full professors at two-year colleges made a median of $58,000.

Work Environment

Psychologists work under many different conditions. Those who work as college or university teachers usually have offices in a building on campus and access to a laboratory in which they carry out experiments.

Offices of school psychologists may be located in the school system headquarters. They may see students and their parents at those offices, or they might work in space set aside for them in several schools within the school district that they may visit regularly.

Psychologists in military service serve in this country or overseas. They may be stationed in Washington, DC, and assigned to an office job, or they may be stationed with other military personnel at a post or, more likely, in a military hospital.

Psychologists employed in government work in such diverse places as public health or vocational rehabilitation agencies, the Department of Veterans Affairs, the Peace Corps, the U.S. Office of Education, or a state department of education. Their working conditions depend largely on the kind of jobs they have. They may be required to travel a lot or to produce publications. They may work mainly with people or be assigned entirely to research.

Some psychologists are self-employed. Most work as clinical psychologists and have offices where they see clients. Others work as consultants to business firms. Self-employed psychologists rent or own their office spaces and arrange their own work schedules.

To be a psychologist, one must have a desire to help people understand themselves and others. A basic curiosity is required as well as a fascination with the way the human mind works.

Outlook

The Bureau of Labor Statistics projects that employment for psychologists will grow about as fast as the average through 2008, with the largest increase in industrial/organizational jobs and the largest decrease in hospital jobs. Increased emphasis on health maintenance and illness prevention as well as growing interest in psychological services for special groups, such as children or the elderly, will create demand for psychologists. Many of these areas depend on government funding, however, and could be adversely affected in an economic downswing when spending is likely to be curtailed. Many openings should be available in business and industry, and the outlook is very good for psychologists who are in full-time independent practice.

Unemployment among new psychologists with doctorate degrees is low. According to the American Psychological Association, approximately two-thirds of those with doctorate degrees had jobs within three months of graduation in 1997. Other statistics revealed that 61 percent of new graduates with Ph.D.s were working in the health service provider subfields of counseling, school, and clinical psychology in 1999.

Prospects look best for doctorate holders in applied areas, such as clinical, counseling, health, and industrial/organizational psychology, and for those with extensive technical training in quantitative research methods and computer applications. Post-doctorates are becoming increasingly crucial in the fields of research psychology that deal with behavior based on biology.

Competition for jobs will be tougher for those with master's or bachelor's degrees. Most job candidates with bachelor's degrees, in fact, will not be able to find employment in the psychology field beyond assistants-level jobs at such places as rehabilitation centers. Some may work as high school psychology teachers if they meet state teaching certification requirements.

For More Information

For information on specialty certification, contact:

American Board of Professional Psychology
514 East Capitol Avenue
Jefferson City, MO 65101
Tel: 573-634-5607
Email: office@abpp.org
Web: http://www.abpp.org

For more on careers in psychology, mental health issues, and ordering books such as **Career Paths in Psychology: Where Your Degree Can Take You,** *contact:*

American Psychological Association
750 First Street, NE
Washington, DC 20002-4242
Tel: 800-374-2721
Web: http://www.apa.org

For more information on becoming a school psychologist, including graduate school information, contact:

National Association of School Psychologists
4340 East-West Highway, Suite 402
Bethesda, MD 20814
Tel: 301-657-0270
Web: http://www.nasponline.org

For licensing information, visit the following Web site:

Association of State and Provincial Psychology Boards
Web: http://www.asppb.org

For a list of Canadian psychology departments providing graduate programs, contact:

Canadian Psychological Association
151 Rue Slater Street, Suite 205
Ottawa, ON K1P 5H3 Canada
Tel: 888-472-0657
Web: http://www.cpa.ca/

Recreational Therapists

Biology Psychology	School Subjects
Helping/teaching Technical/scientific	Personal Skills
Indoors and outdoors Primarily one location	Work Environment
Bachelor's degree	Minimum Education Level
$16,380 to $27,760 to $65,000	Salary Range
Required by certain states	Certification or Licensing
About as fast as the average	Outlook

Overview

Recreational therapists plan, organize, direct, and monitor medically approved recreation programs for patients in hospitals, clinics, and various community settings. These therapists use recreational activities to assist patients with mental, physical, or emotional disabilities to achieve the maximum possible functional independence.

History

The field of therapy has expanded in the past few decades to include recreational therapy as a form of medical treatment. Its use grew out of the realization that soldiers suffering from battle fatigue, shock, and emotional trauma respond positively to organized recreation and activity programs.

As a result, people in nursing homes, hospitals, mental institutions, and adult-care facilities are no longer limited to physical therapy. Experiments have shown that recovery is aided by recreational activities such as sports, music, art, gardening, dance, drama, field trips, and other pastimes. Elderly people are more healthy and alert when their days are filled with activities, field trips, and social get-togethers. People with disabilities can gain greater self-confidence and awareness of their own abilities when they get involved with sports, crafts, and other activities. People recovering from drug or alcohol addiction can reaffirm their self-worth through directed, enjoyable hobbies, clubs, and sports. The recreational therapist is a health professional who organizes these types of activities and helps patients take an active role in their own recovery.

The Job

Recreational therapists work with people who are mentally, physically, or emotionally disabled. They are professionals who employ leisure activities as a form of treatment, much as other health practitioners use surgery, drugs, nutrition, exercise, or psychotherapy. Recreational therapists strive to minimize patients' symptoms, restore function, and improve their physical, mental, and emotional well-being. Enhancing the patient's ability to take part in everyday life is the primary goal of recreational therapy; interesting and rewarding activities are the means for working toward that goal.

Recreational therapists work in a number of different settings, including mental hospitals, psychiatric day hospitals, community mental health centers, nursing homes, adult day care programs, residential facilities for the mentally disabled, school systems, and prisons. They can work as individual staff members, as independent consultants, or as part of a larger therapeutic team. They may get personally involved with patients, or direct the work of assistants and support staff.

The recreational therapist first confers with the doctors, psychiatrists, social workers, physical therapists, and other professionals on staff to coordinate their efforts in treatment. The recreational therapist needs to understand the nature of the patient's ailment, current physical and mental capacities, emotional state, and prospects for recovery. The patient's family and friends are also consulted to find out the patient's interests and hobbies. With this information, the recreational therapist then plans an agenda of activities for that person.

To enrich the lives of people in hospitals and other institutions, recreational therapists use imagination and skill in organizing beneficial activities. Sports, games, arts and crafts, movie screenings, field trips, hobby clubs, and dramatics are only a few examples of activities that can enrich the lives of patients.

Some therapists specialize in certain areas. *Dance/movement therapists* plan and conduct dance and body movement exercises to improve patients' physical and mental well-being. *Art therapists* work with patients in various art methods, such as drawing, painting, and ceramics, as part of their therapeutic and recovery programs. Therapists may also work with pets and other animals, such as horses. *Music therapists* design programs for patients that can involve solo or group singing, playing in bands, rhythmic and other creative activities, listening to music, or attending concerts. Even flowers and gardening can prove beneficial to patients, as is proved by the work of *horticultural therapists*. When the treatment team feels that regular employment would help certain patients, the *industrial therapist* arranges a productive job for the patient in an actual work environment, one that will have the greatest therapeutic value based on the patient's needs and abilities. *Orientation therapists* for the blind work with people who have recently lost their sight, helping them to readjust to daily living and independence through training and exercise. All of these professional therapists plan their programs to meet the needs and capabilities of patients. They also carefully monitor and record each patient's progress and report it to the other members of the medical team.

As part of their jobs, recreational therapists need to understand their patients and set goals for their progress accordingly. A patient having trouble socializing, for example, may have an interest in playing chess, but be overwhelmed by the prospect of actually playing, since that involves interaction with another person. A therapist would proceed slowly, first letting the patient observe a number of games and then assigning a therapeutic assistant to serve as a chess partner for weeks or even months, as long as it takes for the patient to gain enough confidence to seek out other patients for chess partners. The therapist makes a note of the patient's response, modifies the therapy program accordingly, and lets other professionals know of the results. If a patient is responding more enthusiastically to the program, working more cooperatively with others, or is becoming more disruptive, the therapist must note these reactions and periodically reevaluate the patient's activity program.

Responsibilities and elements of the job can vary, depending on the setting in which the recreational therapist works. In nursing homes, the therapist often groups residents according to common or shared interests and ability levels and then plans field trips, parties, entertainment, and other group activities. The therapist documents residents' responses to the activities and continually searches for ways of heightening residents' enjoyment of recreational and leisure activities, not just in the facility but in the surrounding community as well. Because nursing home residents are likely to remain in the facility for months or even years, the activities program makes a big difference in the quality of their lives. Without the stimulation of interesting events to look forward to and participate in, the daily routine of a nursing home can become monotonous and depressing, and some residents are apt to deteriorate both mentally and physically. In some nursing homes, recreational therapists direct the activities program. In others, *activities coordinators* plan and carry out the program under the part-time supervision of a consultant who is either a recreational or *occupational therapist.*

The therapist in a community center might work in a day-care program for the elderly or in a program for mentally disabled adults operated by a county recreation department. No matter what the disability, recreational therapists in community settings face the added logistical challenge of arranging transportation and escort services, if necessary, for prospective participants. Coordinating transportation is less of a problem in hospitals and nursing homes, where the patients all live under one roof. Developing therapeutic recreation programs in community settings requires a large measure of organizational ability, flexibility, and ingenuity.

Recreational therapy is a relatively new field, but it is already a respected, integral part of the treatment of many elderly and disabled people. Clients often need extra encouragement and support to stay active and build on the things they can, rather than can't, do. The activity programs that recreational therapists design and operate can add immeasurable enjoyment to the lives of patients. Beyond this, the activities provide opportunities for exercise and social interaction and may also help relieve anxiety and loneliness, build confidence, and promote each patient's independence.

Requirements

High School

Interested high school students should follow a college preparatory program. Recommended courses include biology and other sciences, English, speech, mathematics, psychology, physical education, art, music, and drama. Verbal and written communication skills are essential because of the interaction with people and the report writing that the job requires.

Postsecondary Training

A bachelor's degree is required for employment as a recreational therapist. More than 150 academic programs in this field are offered at colleges and universities in the United States. Four-year programs include courses in both natural science, such as biology, behavioral science, and human anatomy, and social science, such as psychology and sociology. Courses more specific to the profession include programming for special populations; rehabilitative techniques including self-help skills, mobility, signing for the deaf, and orientation for the blind; medical equipment; current treatment approaches; legal issues; and professional ethics. Students also take recreation courses and are required to serve 360 hours of internship under the supervision of a certified therapeutic recreation specialist.

Continuing education is increasingly becoming a requirement for professionals in this field. Many therapists attend conferences and seminars and take additional university courses. Those with degrees in related fields can enter the profession by earning master's degrees in therapeutic recreation. Advanced degrees are advisable for those seeking advancement to supervisory, administrative, and teaching positions. These requirements will become more strict as more professionals enter the field.

Certification or Licensing

A number of states regulate the profession of therapeutic recreation. Licensing is required in some states; professional certification (or eligibility for certification) is required in others; while titling is regulated in some states and facilities. In other states, many hospitals and other employers require recreational therapists to be certified. Certification for recreational therapists is available through the National Council for Therapeutic Recreation, which awards credentials for therapeutic recreation specialists and assistants. Recreation therapists must check requirements for the states in which they want to work as well as requirements for different types of facilities.

Several other professional organizations offer continuing education classes and additional benefits to professional members. These include the National Therapeutic Recreation Society; the American Therapeutic Recreation Association; and the American Alliance for Health, Physical Education, Recreation, and Dance. These groups also work to improve the salaries and working conditions of the people in the profession.

Exploring

Students interested in recreational therapy can find part-time work as a sports coach or referee, park supervisor, or camp counselor. Volunteer work in a nursing home, hospital, or care facility for disabled adults is also a good way to learn about the daily realities of institutional living. These types of facilities are always looking for volunteers to work with and visit patients. Working with people with physical, mental, or emotional disabilities can be stressful, and volunteer work is a good way for a prospective therapist to test whether they can handle this kind of stress.

Employers

Recreational therapists hold about 39,000 jobs, according to the U.S. Department of Labor. About 38 percent of these people work in nursing homes. Other employers include residential facilities and substance abuse centers, and some therapists are self-employed. Employment opportunities also exist in long-term rehabilitation, home health care, correctional facilities, psychiatric facilities, and transitional programs.

Starting Out

There are many methods for finding out about available jobs in recreational therapy. A good place to start is the job notices and want ads printed in the local newspapers, bulletins from state park and recreation societies, and publications of the professional associations previously mentioned. State employment agencies and human service departments will know of job openings in state hospitals. College placement offices might also be able to put new recreational therapy graduates in touch with prospective employers. Internship programs are sometimes available, offering good opportunities to find potential full-time jobs.

Recent graduates should also make appointments to meet potential employers personally. Most colleges and universities offer career counseling services. Most employers will make themselves available to discuss their programs and the possibility of hiring extra staff. They may also guide new graduates to other institutions currently hiring therapists. Joining professional associations, both state and national, and attending conferences are good ways to meet potential employers and colleagues.

Advancement

Newly graduated recreational therapists generally begin as staff therapists. Advancement is chiefly to supervisory or administrative positions, usually after some years of experience and continuing education. Some therapists teach, conduct research, or do consulting work on a contract basis; a graduate degree is essential for moving into these areas.

Many therapists continue their education but prefer to continue working with patients. For variety, they may choose to work with new groups of people or get a job in a new setting, such as moving from a retirement home to a facility for the disabled. Some may also move to a related field, such as special education, or sales positions involving products and services related to recreational therapy.

Earnings

Salaries of recreational therapists vary according to employment setting, educational background, experience, and region of the country. Recreational therapists earned median salaries of $27,760 in 1998, according to the *Occupational Outlook Handbook*. The lowest ten percent earned less than $16,380 a year, while the highest ten percent earned more than $42,440 annually. Supervisors earned top salaries of $50,000 per year; administrators reported maximum earnings of $65,000 per year; and some consultants and educators reported even higher earnings. Recreational therapists employed by hospitals earned median salaries of $29,700 in 1997, while those employed by personal care and nursing facilities earned $21,900 annually.

Therapists employed at hospitals, clinics, and other facilities generally enjoy a full benefit package, including health insurance and vacation, holiday, and sick pay. Consultants and self-employed therapists must provide their own benefits.

Work Environment

Working conditions vary, but recreational therapists generally work in a ward, a specially equipped activity room, or at a nursing home, a communal room or hall. In a community setting, recreational therapists may interview subjects and plan activities in an office, but they might be in a gymnasium, swimming pool, playground, or outdoors on a nature walk when leading activities. Therapists may also work on horse ranches, farms, and other outdoor facilities catering to people with disabilities.

The job may be physically tiring because therapists are often on their feet all day and may have to lift and carry equipment. Recreational therapists generally work a standard 40-hour week, although weekend and evening hours may be required. Supervisors may have to work overtime, depending on their workload.

Outlook

The U.S. Department of Labor predicts that employment for recreational therapists will grow about as fast as the average through 2008. Increased life expectancies of the elderly and people with developmental disabilities, such as Down's syndrome will create opportunities for recreational therapists. Significant growth is also projected for therapists who work with the physically and mentally handicapped. The incidence of alcohol and drug dependency problems is also growing, creating a demand for qualified therapists to work in short-term alcohol and drug abuse clinics.

Most openings for recreational therapists will be in nursing homes because of the increasing numbers and greater longevity of the elderly. There is also greater public pressure to regulate and improve the quality of life in retirement centers, which may mean more jobs and increased scrutiny of recreational therapists.

Growth in hospital jobs is not expected to be great. Many of the new jobs created will be in hospital-based adult day care programs or in units offering short-term mental health services. Because of economic and social factors, no growth is expected in public mental hospitals. Many of the programs and services formerly offered there are being shifted to community residential facilities for the disabled. Community programs for special populations are expected to expand significantly through 2008.

For More Information

For career information and resources, contact the following organizations:

American Association for Leisure and Recreation
1900 Association Drive
Reston, VA 20191
Tel: 703-476-3472
Email: aal@aahperd.org
Web: http://www.aahperd.org/aalr/

American Therapeutic Recreation Association
1414 Prince Street, Suite 204
Alexandria, VA 22314
Tel: 703-683-9420
Web: http://www.atra-tr.org

National Therapeutic Recreation Society
22377 Belmont Ridge Road
Ashburn, VA 20148
Tel: 703-858-0784
Email: ntrsnrpa@aol.com
Web: http://www.nrpa.org/branches/ntrs.htm

For information on certification, contact:

National Council for Therapeutic Recreation Certification
7 Elmwood Drive
New City, NY 10956
Tel: 845-639-1439
Email: nctrc@nctrc.org
Web: http://www.nctrc.org

Rehabilitation Counselors

Psychology Sociology	School Subjects
Helping/teaching Technical/scientific	Personal Skills
Primarily indoors Primarily one location	Work Environment
Bachelor's degree	Minimum Education Level
$20,000 to $50,000 to $65,000	Salary Range
Recommended	Certification or Licensing
Faster than the average	Outlook

Overview

Rehabilitation counselors provide counseling and guidance services to people with disabilities to help them resolve life problems and to train for and locate work that is suitable to their physical and mental abilities, interests, and aptitudes.

History

Today it is generally accepted that people with disabilities can and should have the opportunity to become as fully independent as possible in all aspects of life, from school to work to social activities. In response to the needs of disabled war veterans, Congress passed the first Vocational Rehabilitation Act in 1920. The act set in place the Vocational Rehabilitation

Program, a federal-state program that provides for the delivery of rehabilitation services, including counseling, to eligible people with disabilities.

The profession of rehabilitation counseling has its roots in the Rehabilitation Act, which allowed for funds to train personnel. What was at first a job title developed into a fully recognized profession as it became evident that the delivery of effective rehabilitation services required highly trained specialists. Early efforts for providing rehabilitation counseling and other services were often directed especially toward the nation's veterans. In 1930, the Veterans Administration was created to supply support services to veterans and their families, and in 1989, the U.S. Department of Veterans Affairs was created as the 14th cabinet department in the U.S. government.

The passage of the Americans with Disabilities Act in 1990 recognized the rights and needs of people with disabilities and developed federal regulations and guidelines aimed at eliminating discrimination and other barriers preventing people with disabilities from participating fully in school, workplace, and public life. Many state and federal programs have since been created to aid people with disabilities.

The Job

Rehabilitation counselors work with people with disabilities to identify barriers to medical, psychological, personal, social, and vocational adjustment and to develop a plan of action to remove or reduce those barriers.

Clients are referred to rehabilitation programs from many sources. Sometimes they seek help on their own initiative; sometimes their families bring them in. They may be referred by a physician, hospital, or social worker, or they may be sent by employment agencies, schools, or accident commissions. A former employer may seek help for the individual.

The counselor's first step is to determine the nature and extent of the disability and evaluate how that disability interferes with work and other life functions. This determination is made from medical and psychological reports as well as from family history, educational background, work experience, and other evaluative information.

The next step is to determine a vocational direction and plan of services to overcome the handicaps to employment or independent living.

The rehabilitation counselor coordinates a comprehensive evaluation of a client's physical functioning abilities and vocational interests, aptitudes, and skills. This information is used to develop for the client a vocational or independent-living goal and the services necessary to reach that goal. Services that the rehabilitation counselor may coordinate or provide include physical and mental restoration, academic or vocational training, vocational counseling, job analysis, job modification or reasonable accommodation, and job placement. Limited financial assistance in the form of maintenance or transportation assistance may also be provided.

The counselor's relationship with the client may be as brief as a week or as long as several years, depending on the nature of the problem and the needs of the client.

Requirements

High School

High school students interested in rehabilitation counseling should enroll in a college preparatory course, including sociology, biology, English, speech, mathematics, psychology, and social studies.

Postsecondary Training

Although there are some positions available for people with a bachelor's degree in rehabilitation counseling, a master's degree in rehabilitation counseling, counseling and guidance, or counseling psychology is preferred for those entering the field. Preparation for a master's degree program requires an undergraduate major in behavioral sciences, social sciences, or a related field or the completion of an undergraduate degree program in rehabilitation counseling. This degree is offered at more than 30 colleges and universities in the United States. Students preparing for this career should take courses in sociology, psychology, physiology, history, and statistics as well as courses in English and communications. Several universities now offer courses in various aspects of physical therapy and special education training. Students also should consider courses in sign language and speech therapy. Foreign language skills are also helpful in this field.

The master's degree program in rehabilitation counseling is usually a two-year program. There are graduate programs in rehabilitation counseling in many large universities. The program includes courses in medical aspects of disability, psychosocial aspects of disability, testing techniques, statistics, personality theory, personality development, abnormal psychology, techniques of counseling, occupational information, and vocational training and job placement. More than 75 graduate programs in rehabilitation counseling have been accredited by the Council on Rehabilitation Education.

Certification or Licensing

Most state government rehabilitation agencies require future counselors to meet state civil service and merit system rules. The applicant must take a competitive written examination and may also have an individual interview and evaluation by a special board.

Many employers now require their rehabilitation counselors to be certified by the Commission on Rehabilitation Counselor Certification (CRCC). The purpose of certification is to provide assurance that professionals engaged in rehabilitation counseling meet acceptable standards and maintain those standards through continuing education. To become certified, counselors must pass an extensive written examination to demonstrate their knowledge of rehabilitation counseling. The CRCC requires the master's degree as the minimum educational level for certification. Applicants who meet these certification requirements receive the Certified Rehabilitation Counselor credential.

In about 45 states, counselors in private practice must be licensed by the state. Licensing requirements vary by state; however, not all states include rehabilitation counselors under state regulatory boards.

Other Requirements

The most important personal attribute required for rehabilitation counseling is the ability to get along well with other people. Rehabilitation counselors work with many different kinds of clients and must be able to see situations and problems from the client's point of view. They must be both patient and persistent. Rehabilitation may be a slow process with many delays and setbacks. The counselor must maintain a calm, positive manner even when no progress is made.

Exploring

Students considering a career with disabled people should seek opportunities to work in this field. They may volunteer to work as a counselor at a disabled children's camp. They also may volunteer with a local vocational rehabilitation agency or a facility such as the Easter Seal Society or Goodwill. Students may be able to read to the blind or teach a hobby to someone who has been disabled by accident or illness.

Employers

Rehabilitation counselors work in a variety of settings. About three-quarters of rehabilitation counselors work for state agencies; some also work for local and federal agencies. Employment opportunities are available in rehabilitation centers, mental health agencies, developmental disability agencies, sheltered workshops, training institutions, and special schools.

Starting Out

School placement offices are the best places for the new graduate to begin the career search. In addition, the National Rehabilitation Counseling Association and the American Rehabilitation Counseling Association (a division of the American Counseling Association) are sources for employment information. The new counselor may also apply directly to agencies for available positions. State and local vocational rehabilitation agencies employ about ten thousand rehabilitation counselors. The Department of Veterans Affairs employs several hundred people to assist with the rehabilitation of disabled veterans. Many rehabilitation counselors are employed by private for-profit or nonprofit rehabilitation programs and facilities. Others are employed in industry, schools, hospitals, and other settings, while others are self-employed.

Advancement

The rehabilitation counselor will usually receive regular salary increases after gaining experience in the job. He or she may move from relatively easy cases to increasingly challenging ones. Counselors may advance into such positions as administrator or supervisor after several years of counseling experience. It is also possible to find related counseling and teaching positions, which may represent an advancement in other fields.

Earnings

Information about salaries for rehabilitation counselors is limited. Salaries vary widely according to each state and community. Starting salaries tend to average around $20,000 per year, and rehabilitation counselors with many years of experience can earn up to $50,000 per year. Those in supervisory and administrative positions can earn up to $65,000 per year. Self-employed counselors with established practices generally earn the highest salaries.

Rehabilitation counselors employed by the federal government generally start at the GS-9 or GS-11 level. In 2001, basic GS-9 salary was $33,254. Those with master's degrees generally began at the GS-11 level, with a salary of $40,236 in 2001. Salaries for federal government workers vary according to the region of the country in which they work. Those working in areas with a higher cost of living receive additional locality pay.

Counselors employed by government and private agencies and institutions generally receive health insurance, pension plans, and other benefits, including vacation, sick, and holiday pay. Self-employed counselors must provide their own benefits.

Work Environment

Rehabilitation counselors work approximately 40 hours each week and do not usually have to work during evenings or weekends. They work both in the office and in the field. Depending on the type of training required, lab space and workout or therapy rooms may be available. Rehabilitation counselors must usually keep detailed accounts of their progress with clients and write reports. They may spend many hours traveling about the community to visit employed clients, prospective employers, trainees, or training programs.

Outlook

The passage of the Americans with Disabilities Act of 1990 has increased the demand for rehabilitation counselors, as more local, state, and federal programs are initiated that are designed to assist people with disabilities, and as private institutions and companies seek to comply with this new legislation. Budget pressures may serve to limit the number of new rehabilitation counselors to be hired by government agencies, however, the overall outlook remains excellent.

For More Information

For general information on careers in rehabilitation counseling, contact:

American Rehabilitation Counseling Association
5999 Stevenson Avenue
Alexandria, VA 22304-3300
Tel: 800-545-2223
Web: http://www.nchrtm.okstate.edu/ARCA/

For information on certification, contact:

Commission on Rehabilitation Counselor Certification
1835 Rohlwing Road, Suite E
Rolling Meadows, IL 60008
Tel: 847-394-2104
Web: http://www.crccertification.org

For information on credentialing and education, contact:

National Rehabilitation Counseling Association
8807 Sudley Road, Suite 102
Manassas, VA 22110-4719
Tel: 703-361-2077
Email: NRCAOFFICE@aol.com
Web: http://nrca-net.org/

Social Workers

Health Psychology	School Subjects
Communication/ideas Helping/teaching	Personal Skills
Primarily indoors Primarily multiple locations	Work Environment
Bachelor's degree	Minimum Education Level
$19,250 to $30,590 to $49,080+	Salary Range
Required by all states	Certification or Licensing
Much faster than the average	Outlook

Overview

Social workers help people and communities solve problems. These problems include poverty, racism, discrimination, physical and mental illness, addiction, and abuse. They counsel individuals and families, they lead group sessions, they research social problems, and they develop policy and programs. Social workers are dedicated to empowering people and helping people to preserve their dignity and worth.

History

Even before the United States became a country, poverty and unemployment were among society's problems. Almshouses and shelters that provided the homeless with jobs and rooms were established as early as 1657. The social work profession as we know it today, however, has its origins in the "friendly visitor" of the early 1800s; these charity workers went from home to home offering guidance in how to move beyond the troubles of poverty.

At a time when not much financial assistance was available from local governments, the poor relied on friendly visitors for instruction on household budgeting and educating their children. Despite their good intentions, however, the friendly visitors could not provide the poor with all the necessary support. The middle-class women who served as friendly visitors were generally far removed from the experiences of the lower classes. Most of the friendly visitors served the community for only a very short time and therefore did not have the opportunity to gain much experience with the poor. The great difference between the life experiences of the friendly visitors and the experiences of their clients sometimes resulted in serious problems: the self-esteem and ambitions of the poor were sometimes damaged by the moral judgments of the friendly visitors. In some cases, friendly visitors served only to promote their middle-class values and practices. By the late 1800s, many charitable organizations developed in U.S. and Canadian cities. With the development of these organizations came a deeper insight into improving the conditions of the poor. Serving as a friendly visitor came to be considered an apprenticeship; it became necessary for friendly visitors to build better relationships with their clients. Friendly visitors were encouraged to take the time to learn about their clients and to develop an understanding of each client's individual needs. Nevertheless, some sense of moral superiority remained, as these charitable organizations refused assistance to alcoholics, beggars, and prostitutes.

The birth of the settlement house brought charity workers even closer to their clients. Settlement houses served as communities for the poor and were staffed by young, well-educated idealists anxious to solve society's problems. The staff people lived among their clients and learned from them. In 1889, Jane Addams established the best known of the settlement houses, a community in Chicago called Hull House. Addams wrote extensively of the problems of the poor, and her efforts to provide solutions led to the foundation of social work education. She emphasized the importance of an education specific to the concerns of the social worker. By the 1920s, social work master's degree programs were established in many universities.

Theories and methodologies of social work have changed over the years, but the basis of the profession has remained the same: helping people and addressing social problems. As society changes, so do its problems, calling for redefinition of the social work profession. The first three fields of formal social work were defined by setting: medical social work; psychiatric social work; and child welfare. Later, practice was classified by different methodologies: casework; group work; and community organization. Most recently, the social work profession has been divided into two areas—direct practice and indirect practice.

The Job

After months of physical abuse from her husband, a young woman has taken her children and moved out of her house. With no job and no home, and fearing for her safety, she looks for a temporary shelter for herself and her children. Once there, she can rely on the help of social workers who will provide her with a room, food, and security. The social workers will offer counseling and emotional support to help her address the problems in her life. They will involve her in group sessions with other victims of abuse. They will direct her to job training programs and other employment services. They will set up interviews with managers of low-income housing. As the woman makes efforts to improve her life, the shelter will provide day care for the children. All these resources exist because the social work profession has long been committed to empowering people and improving society.

The social worker's role extends even beyond the shelter. If the woman has trouble getting help from other agencies, the social worker will serve as an advocate, stepping in to ensure that she gets the aid to which she is entitled. The woman may also qualify for long-term assistance from the shelter, such as a second-step program in which a social worker offers counseling and other support over several months. The woman's individual experience will also help in the social worker's research of the problem of domestic violence; with that research, the social worker can help the community come to a better understanding of the problem and can direct society toward solutions. Some of these solutions may include the development of special police procedures for domestic disputes, or court-ordered therapy groups for abusive spouses.

Direct social work practice is also known as clinical practice. As the name suggests, direct practice involves working directly with the client by offering counseling, advocacy, information and referral, and education. Indirect practice concerns the structures through which the direct practice is offered. Indirect practice (a practice consisting mostly of social workers with Ph.D.s) involves program development and evaluation, administration, and policy analysis. Of the 134,200 members of the National Association of Social Workers, 69 percent work in direct service roles and 19 percent in indirect roles.

Because of the number of problems facing individuals, families and communities, social workers find jobs in a variety of settings and with a variety of client groups. Some of these areas are discussed in the following paragraphs:

Health/mental health care social workers. Mental health care has become the lead area of social work employment. These jobs are competitive and typically go to more experienced social workers. Settings include community mental health centers, where social workers serve persistently mentally ill people and participate in outreach services; state and county mental hospitals, for long-term, inpatient care; facilities of the Department of Veterans Affairs, involving a variety of mental health care programs for veterans; and private psychiatric hospitals, for patients who can pay directly. Social workers also work with patients who have physical illnesses. They help individuals and their families adjust to the illness and the changes that illness may bring to their lives. They confer with physicians and with other members of the medical team to make plans about the best way to help the patient. They explain the treatment and its anticipated outcome to both the patient and the family. They help the patient adjust to the possible prospect of long hospitalization and isolation from the family.

Child care/family services social workers. Efforts are being made to offer a more universal system of care that would incorporate child care, family services, and community service. Child care services include day care homes, child care centers, and Head Start centers. Social workers in this setting attempt to address all the problems children face from infancy to late adolescence. They work with families to detect problems early and intervene when necessary. They research the problems confronting children and families, and they establish new services or adapt existing services to address these problems. They provide parenting education to teenage parents, which can involve living with a teenage mother in a foster care situation, teaching parenting skills, and caring for the baby while the mother attends school. Social workers alert employers to employees' needs for daytime child care.

Social workers in this area of service are constantly required to address new issues; in recent years, for example, social workers have developed services for families composed of different cultural backgrounds, services for children with congenital disabilities resulting from the mother's drug use, and disabilities related to HIV or AIDS.

Geriatric social workers. Within this field, social workers provide individual and family counseling services in order to assess the older person's needs and strengths. Social workers help older people locate transportation and housing services. They also offer adult day care services, or adult foster care services that match older people with families. Adult protective services protect older people from abuse and neglect, and respite services allow family members time off from the care of an older person. A little-recognized problem is the rising incidence of AIDS among the elderly; 10 percent of all AIDS patients are aged 50 or over.

School social workers. In schools, social workers serve students and their families, teachers, administrators, and other school staff members. Education, counseling, and advocacy are important aspects of school social work. With education, social workers attempt to prevent alcohol and drug abuse, teen pregnancy, and the spread of AIDS and other sexually transmitted diseases. They provide multicultural and family life education. They counsel students who are discriminated against because of their sexual orientation or racial, ethnic, or religious background. They also serve as advocates for these students, bringing issues of discrimination before administrators, school boards, and student councils.

A smaller number of social workers are employed in the areas of social work education (a field composed of the professors and instructors who teach and train students of social work); group practice (in which social workers facilitate treatment and support groups); and corrections (providing services to inmates in penal institutions). Social workers also offer counseling, occupational assistance, and advocacy to those with addictions and disabilities, to the homeless, and to women, children, and the elderly who have been in abusive situations.

Client groups expand and change as societal problems change. Social work professionals must remain aware of the problems affecting individuals and communities in order to offer assistance to as many people as possible.

Computers have become important tools for social workers. Client records are maintained on computers, allowing for easier collection and analysis of data. Interactive computer programs are used in training social workers, as well as to analyze case histories (such as for an individual's risk of HIV infection).

Requirements

High School

To prepare for social work, you should take courses in high school that will improve your communication skills, such as English, speech, and composition. On a debate team, you could further develop your skills in communication as well as research and analysis. History, social studies, and sociology courses are important in understanding the concerns and issues of society. Although some work is available for those with only a high school diploma or associate's degree (as a social work aide or social services technician), the most opportunities exist for people with degrees in social work.

Postsecondary Training

The Council on Social Work Education requires that five areas be covered in accredited bachelor's degree social work programs: human behavior and the social environment; social welfare policy and services; social work practice; research; and field practicum. Most programs require two years of liberal arts study followed by two years of study in the social work major. Also, students must complete a field practicum of at least 400 hours. Graduates of these programs can find work in public assistance or they can work with the elderly or with people with mental or developmental disabilities.

Although no clear lines of classification are drawn in the social work profession, most supervisory and administrative positions require at least a master's degree in social work (M.S.W.). Master's programs are organized according to fields of practice (such as mental health care), problem areas (substance abuse), population groups (the elderly), and practice roles (practice with individuals, families, or communities). They are usually two-year programs, with at least 900 hours of field practice. Most positions in mental health care facilities require an M.S.W. Doctoral degrees are also available and prepare students for research and teaching. Most social workers with doctorates go to work in community organizations.

Certification or Licensing

Licensing, certification, or registration of social workers is required by all states. To receive the necessary licensing, a social worker will typically have to gain a certain amount of experience and also pass an exam. Five voluntary certification programs help to identify those social workers who have gained the knowledge and experience necessary to meet national standards.

Other Requirements

Social work requires great dedication. As a social worker, you have the responsibility of helping whole families, groups, and communities, as well as focusing on the needs of individuals. Your efforts will not always be supported by the society at large; sometimes you must work against a community's prejudice, disinterest, and denial. You must also remain sensitive to the problems of your clients, offering support, and not moral judgment or personal bias. The only way to effectively address new social problems and new client groups is to remain open to the thoughts and needs of all human beings. Assessing situations and solving problems requires clarity of vision and a genuine concern for the well-being of others.

With this clarity of vision, your work will be all the more rewarding. Social workers have the satisfaction of making a connection with other people and helping them through difficult times. Along with the rewards, however, the work can provide a great deal of stress. Hearing repeatedly about the deeply troubled lives of prison inmates, the mentally ill, abused women and children, and others can be depressing and defeating. Trying to convince society of the need for changes in laws and services can be a long, hard struggle. You must have perseverance to fight for your clients against all odds.

Exploring

As a high school student, you may find openings for summer or part-time work as a receptionist or file clerk with a local social service agency. If there is no opportunity for paid employment, you could work as a volunteer. Good experience is also provided by work as a counselor in a camp for children with physical, mental, or developmental disabilities. Your local YMCA, park district, or other recreational facility may need volunteers for group recreation programs, including programs designed for the prevention of delinquency. By reporting for your high school newspaper, you'll have the opportunity to interview people, conduct surveys, and research social change, all of which are important aspects of the social work profession.

You could also volunteer a few afternoons a week to read to people in retirement homes or to the blind. Work as a tutor in special education programs is sometimes available to high school students.

Employers

Social workers can be employed in direct or clinical practice, providing individual and family counseling services, or they may work as administrators for the organizations that provide direct practice. Social workers are employed by community health and mental health centers; hospitals and mental hospitals; child care, family services, and community service organizations, including day care and Head Start programs; elderly care programs, including adult protective services and adult day care and foster care; prisons; shelters and halfway houses; schools; courts; and nursing homes.

Starting Out

Most students of social work pursue a master's degree and in the process learn about the variety of jobs available. They also make valuable connections through faculty and other students. Through the university's job placement service or an internship program, a student will learn about job openings and potential employers.

A social work education in an accredited program will provide you with the most opportunities, and the best salaries and chances for promotion, but practical social work experience can also earn you full-time employment. A part-time job or volunteer work will introduce you to social work professionals who can provide you with career guidance and letters of reference. Agencies with limited funding may not be able to afford to hire social workers with M.S.W.s and will therefore look for applicants with a great deal of experience and lower salary expectations.

Advancement

The attractive and better-paying jobs tend to go to those with more years of practical experience. Dedication to your job, an extensive resume, and good references will lead to advancement in the profession. Also, many social work programs offer continuing education workshops, courses, and seminars. These refresher courses help practicing social workers to refine their skills and to learn about new areas of practice and new methods and problems. The courses are intended to supplement your social work education, not substitute for a bachelor's or master's degree. These continuing education courses can lead to job promotions and salary increases.

Earnings

The higher the degree, the more money a social worker can make in the profession. The area of practice also determines earnings; the areas of mental health, group services, and community organization and planning provide higher salaries, while elderly and disabled care generally provide lower pay. Salaries also vary among regions; social workers on the east and west coasts earn higher salaries than those in the Midwest. Earnings in Canada vary from province to province as well. During the first five years of practice, a social worker's salary will increase faster than in later years.

The median salary range for social workers in the United States was approximately $30,590 in 1998, according to the *Occupational Outlook Handbook*. The top 10 percent earned more than $49,080, while the lowest 10 percent earned less than $19,250. Social workers employed by the U.S. government earn an average annual salary of about $45,300. Average salaries in Canada are higher, with a median range of $40,000 to $45,000.

Although women make up a large percentage of the profession, only 2.2 percent of female social workers in the United States receive more than $60,000, as opposed to 6.3 percent of male social workers.

Work Environment

Social workers do not always work at a desk. When they do, they may be interviewing clients, writing reports, or conferring with other staff members. Depending on the size of the agency, office duties such as typing letters, filing, and answering phones may be performed by an aide or volunteer. Social workers employed at shelters or halfway houses may spend most of their time with clients, tutoring, counseling, or leading groups.

Some social workers have to drive to remote areas to make a home visit. They may go into inner city neighborhoods, schools, courts, or jails. In larger cities, domestic violence and homeless shelters are sometimes located in rundown or dangerous areas. Most social workers are involved directly with the people they serve and must carefully examine the client's living conditions and family relations. Although some of these living conditions can be pleasant and demonstrate a good home situation, others can be squalid and depressing.

Advocacy involves work in a variety of different environments. Although much of this work may require making phone calls and sending faxes and letters, it also requires meetings with clients' employers, directors of agencies, local legislators, and others. It may sometimes require testifying in court as well.

Outlook

The field of social work is expected to grow much faster than the average for all occupations through 2008, according to the U.S. Department of Labor. The greatest factor for this growth is the increased number of older people who are in need of social services. Social workers that specialize in gerontology will find many job opportunities in nursing homes, hospitals, and home health care agencies. The needs of the future elderly population are likely to be different from those of the present elderly. Currently, the elderly appreciate community living, while subsequent generations may demand more individual care.

Schools will also need more social workers to deal with issues such as teenage pregnancies, children from single-parent households, and any adjustment problems recent immigrants may have. The trend to integrate students with disabilities into the general school population will require the expertise of social workers to make the transition smoother. However, job availability in schools will depend on funding given by state and local sources.

To help control costs, hospitals are encouraging early discharge for some of their patients. Social workers will be needed by hospitals to help secure health services for patients in their homes. There is also a growing number of people with physical disabilities or impairments staying in their own homes, requiring home health care workers.

Increased availability of health insurance funding and the growing number of people able to pay for professional help will create opportunities for those in private practice. Many businesses hire social workers to help in employee assistance programs, often on a contractual basis.

Poverty is still a main issue addressed by social workers. Families are finding it increasingly challenging to make ends meet on wages that are just barely above the minimum. The problem of fathers who do not make their court-ordered child support payments forces single mothers to work more than one job or rely on welfare. An increased awareness of domestic violence has also pointed up the fact that many of the homeless and unemployed are women who have left abusive situations. Besides all this, working with the poor is often considered unattractive, leaving many social work positions in this area unfilled.

Competition for jobs in urban areas will remain strong. However, there is still a shortage of social workers in rural areas; these areas usually cannot offer the high salaries or modern facilities that attract large numbers of applicants.

The social work profession is constantly changing. The survival of social service agencies, both private and public, depends on shifting political, economic, and workplace issues.

Social work professionals are worried about the threat of declassification. Because of budget constraints and a need for more workers, some agencies have lowered their job requirements. When unable to afford qualified professionals, they hire those with less education and experience. This downgrading raises questions about quality of care and professional standards. Just as in some situations low salaries push out the qualified social worker, so do high salaries. In the area of corrections, attractive salaries (up to $40,000 for someone with a two-year associate's degree) have resulted in more competition from other service workers.

Liability is another growing concern. If a social worker, for example, tries to prove that a child has been beaten or attempts to remove a child from his or her home, the worker can potentially be sued for libel. At the other extreme, a social worker can face criminal charges for failure to remove a child from an abusive home. More social workers are taking out malpractice insurance.

For More Information

For information on social work careers and educational programs, contact:

Council on Social Work Education
1725 Duke Street, Suite 500
Alexandria, VA 22314
Tel: 703-683-8080
Email: info@cswe.org
Web: http://www.cswe.org

To access the online publication, **Choices: Careers in Social Work,** *visit the following Web site:*

National Association of Social Workers
750 First Street, NE, Suite 700
Washington DC 20002-4241
Tel: 800-638-8799
Email: info@naswdc.org
Web: http://www.naswdc.org

Index